MULTILINGUAL MATTERS

Evaluating Bilingual Education: A Canadian Case Study

Merrill Swain and
Sharon Lapkin

The Ontario Institute for Studies in Education

MULTILINGUAL
MATTERS LTD

British Library Cataloguing in Publication Data

Swain, Merrill
    Evaluating bilingual education.
    — (Multilingual matters; 2)
    1. Education, Bilingual — Canada
    I. Title   II. Lapkin, Sharon
    371.97'0971   LC3734

        ISBN 0-905028-10-4
        ISBN 0-905028-09-0 Pbk

Multilingual Matters Ltd,
Bank House, 8a Hill Road,
Clevedon, Avon BS21 7HH,
England.

Typeset by Wayside Graphics, Clevedon, Avon.
Printed in Great Britain by
Short Run Press Ltd, Exeter EX2 7LW.

Contents

List of Figures

List of Tables

Acknowledgements

No major report can be the product of its authors alone. Jill Kamin helped to compile the bibliography, and in doing so demonstrated to us the many advantages of computerized lists. She also typed the manuscript into the computer, making us vow never to type another manuscript without the aid of such modern technological advances. Birgit Harley edited our manuscript and provided insightful comments along the way. Our warmest thanks go to Jill and Birgit for their tireless and constantly cheerful support.

Although we have been its Principal Investigators, the Bilingual Education Project has always been a collaborative effort. Our reports are a result of the team of individuals who have worked together over the years and without whom the research and its outputs would not be the same. We extend our thanks to Christine Andrew, Henri Barik, Gila Hanna, Birgit Harley, Jill Kamin, Grace Lake, Edna Nwanunobi, Kathy McTavish, Kathy Scott, and Lindsay Shanahan for their participation; to Stacy Churchill, Jim Cummins, Adrienne Game, Fred Genesee, and David H. H. Stern for their feedback, and to Charlotte Nadeau for her secretarial involvement.

The report on which this book is based, *Bilingual Education in Ontario: A Decade of Research*, was published in 1981 (Toronto, Ontario: The Ministry of Education, Ontario). The work of the Bilingual Education Project has been funded over the years by the Ministry of Education of the Province of Ontario, and the Office of Research and Development of the Ontario Institute for Studies in Education. We are grateful for their continued support.

Finally, and most important, we want to express our sincere thanks to all the participating school boards, board and school personnel, and especially to the students and their parents for their patience and their co-operation.

1 Introduction

To a considerable extent, debate about bilingual education has focussed on the advantages and/or disadvantages of using a first, second or foreign language(s) for instructional purposes in primary schooling. The outcomes of French immersion education — the topic of this book — indicate that there is nothing inherently impossible, or negative, in providing initial education through the medium of a second or foreign language. As a result, one is forced to examine factors that extend beyond the immediate school environment for explanations of success or failure in school — factors that are rooted in historical, cultural, economic, and political events and that impinge upon the social and psychological life of the individual child. For schools to maximize children's chance of success in the educational system, programs need to be planned and implemented which are sensitive to the conditions of the wider societal context in which the child lives.

In the case of French immersion schooling, the first program in the public sector began as a result of considerable pressure and agitation by a group of English-speaking parents in Quebec whose common concern was that their children become highly proficient in French (LAMBERT & TUCKER, 1972). Their concern about their children's abilities in French reflected the political and economic realities of their environment — that French was being increasingly emphasized as the language of work, and indeed, has since become legalized as the official *langue de travail* in Quebec. At the same time the Federal Government was bilingualizing its services, and the combined impact of the Quebec and Federal governmental policies and rhetoric led to an increased recognition and acceptance among English-Canadians of the value of knowing French. With this heightened awareness of the value (economic, educational, cultural, and political) of learning French, parents and educators across Canada sought educational solutions that would lead to increased proficiency in French. The results from the Quebec French immersion program had just been published (LAMBERT & MACNAMARA, 1969; LAMBERT, JUST & SEGALOWITZ, 1970). For many, this program provided one obvious, but radical solution to their demands that school improve the teaching of French. Since then, the battle for improved French teaching has been led in community after community by parents who were actively interested in their children's education, relentless in their search for documentation supporting immersion education, and articulate in expressing their demands. And, as part of the dominant, majority group (LIEBERSON, 1970), their demands have been heard and implemented. Thus, the very existence of French immersion schooling is the result of political and economic forces, and, in practice provides skills important for members of the majority group in Canada to possess.

For members of the majority group, learning a second language is not likely to pose a threat to a sense of personal or cultural identity, nor to the maintenance of the first language (LAMBERT, 1975). In spite of this, immersion parents wanted to be assured that the development of their children's English language skills would not suffer. Indeed, these parents wanted their children to learn French so long as it was not at the expense of first language literacy or academic achievement. Thus, mother tongue education is an integral part of the program, although in a primary immersion program, it may not be introduced until the third or fourth year of schooling.

Once an immersion program is established in a community, it still remains an optional program. Participation in the program is voluntary, and parents can always choose to enrol their children in the regular English program in the same school or in another school in the same community rather than in an immersion program.

These characteristics — parental pressure and involvement in program initiation and implementation, majority group membership of participants, positive attitudes towards the first and second languages, and the possibility of choice between mother tongue education or bilingual education — have played a significant role in affecting the outcomes of French immersion programs in Canada (SWAIN, 1981d).

Scope of the Study

The purpose of this book is to provide a non-technical synthesis of a decade of research concerning immersion education. This research has been conducted in the context of the Bilingual Education Project in the Modern

Language Centre of the Ontario Institute for Studies in Education (Toronto, Canada). The immersion programs studied over the years include three major alternatives: the early total French immersion programs of the Carleton, Ottawa, and Toronto Boards of Education; the early partial French immersion program of the Elgin County Board of Education; and the late partial French immersion program of the Peel County Board of Education. These three variations are representative of immersion programs found across Ontario and the other Canadian provinces in that they share the following characteristics:

   a) The programs, which are optional, serve a primarily English-speaking school population. At the outset of the program, most students are unilingual.
   b) In the initial year(s) of the program, from one-half to an entire school day is devoted to instruction in French. French is the medium of instruction for all or most school subjects including a language arts period.
   c) Students in immersion programs study the same curriculum content as their peers in the regular English program.

The specific programs that have been evaluated by the Bilingual Education Project are described in detail in Chapter 2. It is important to note that French immersion programs as they exist in Ontario represent one of a variety of possible approaches to bilingual education. In the United States, for example, many bilingual education programs serving students from non-English home languages begin with instruction in the child's first language and move gradually to instruction in English. These programs have been labelled "transitional" bilingual education because a transition is made from the minority language spoken by members of an ethnic group to English, the language of the majority of the population of the United States. Transitional programs are not common in Canada. One finds, however, a few examples of bilingual programs in Ukranian or German (in Alberta), or "heritage language" programs in which a minority language is taught after the school day (in Ontario). The teaching of minority languages indicates a desire to preserve the home language and underlines the perceived value in Canada of languages other than English or French. A more common form of bilingual education in Canada is French immersion education, serving the English-speaking majority by giving students access to French, one of Canada's two official languages.

Current Enrolment

Since the early seventies, the growth in French immersion programs in Ontario has been dramatic. Defining immersion as a program where half or more of the instruction occurs in the second language, Ontario Ministry of Education figures for the 1979–80 academic year show more than 28,000 students enrolled in such programs at the elementary school level (Kindergarten through grade 8). This represents about 2.5% of the total English-speaking student population at these grade levels in the province. Across Canada, the 1981–82 enrolment figures compiled by Canadian Parents for French, show 88,000 students enrolled in these programs, an increase of 12,000 over the previous academic year.

Nature of the Research

In all the Canadian research studies on French immersion, the focus has been on comparing the progress of students enrolled in the experimental programs with that of their peers enrolled in regular English programs. This research emphasis has been motivated by the underlying philosophy of immersion education — that the immersion students' education should be the same as that of students in regular English programs offered in any given school system, with the only major difference being the language through which the teacher and students communicate in the classroom.

Outline of the Study

In the next chapter, an overview of the French immersion programs studied by the Bilingual Education Project is presented, and the characteristics of some other bilingual education programs found in Ontario are summarized. In Chapter 3, the specific research questions addressed in the evaluation are listed and discussed, the research design and procedures are described, and some issues which generally arise in the evaluation of educational programs are explored. The evaluation findings concerning the linguistic outcomes of French immersion programs are presented in Chapter 4, the academic outcomes in Chapter 5, and some social and psychological outcomes in Chapter 6. In these chapters, results from the early total, early partial, and late partial French immersion programs evaluated by the Bilingual Education Project are highlighted, although reference is made to studies of similar bilingual education programs in Ontario and throughout Canada. The final chapter serves as a summary of this book and indicates some implications of the research for policy makers. It is followed by a comprehensive bibliography on immersion education in Canada and the United States.

2 French Immersion Programs in Ontario

In this chapter, the basic principles that underlie immersion education are discussed in general terms, and the specific bilingual programs studied by the Bilingual Education Project are described in some detail.

The Process

The word "process" is used here to refer to what actually goes on in the classroom. What are the instructional principles on which immersion education is based? What are the special features of the teachers' approach in the immersion classroom?

As noted in Chapter 1, immersion education is based on the principle that students receive the same type of education as they would in the regular English program, but that the medium of instruction, the language through which material is presented and discussed, is French. Immersion programs have been described as providing a naturalistic setting for second language acquisition; that is, the second language is acquired in much the same manner as children acquire their first language, by interacting with speakers of the language in authentic and meaningful communicative situations. In both cases, the learner is provided (by the parents or the teacher) with rich language input and gradually begins to use the language in order to communicate. In early immersion settings particularly, the practice in the first and second years of the program is to expose children to a large amount of second language use (by the teacher), but to let them talk among themselves and to the teacher in their home language, English. Thus, as should be the case in any classroom, the teacher accepts and starts from the existing language, interests and skills of the children. As they feel able to, students gradually begin to use French vocabulary items and simple phrases until, in the latter part of grade 1, French is firmly established as the language of the classroom. In late immersion programs however, because the students have studied French in earlier grades through a core French program, the teacher is more likely to insist that French be used in class by the students right from the beginning of the immersion program. (The term "core French" is used across Canada as a label for French as a second language instruction delivered in daily 20- to 40-minute class periods. It is comparable to French as a foreign language classes in many countries.)

Early immersion education began in Canada with the idea that through the exclusive use of French by the teachers in communicating with their students, the second language would be acquired incidentally — incidentally, that is, to learning about the content of what was being communicated. The focus of the teachers has been on conveying the content to their students and on responding to the content of what their students are saying, no matter how they are saying it, or in which language it is being said. Here the importance of being able to understand the child's home language is clear. Were the teachers not able to understand English, they would be unable to respond appropriately to the child's questions or statements. There would then be no meaningful conversations, which are considered to be of crucial importance in language acquisition.

The initial focus, then, in early immersion programs is on developing French language comprehension skills rather than production skills. This follows from the understanding that in natural language acquisition, comprehension precedes (and exceeds) production. Indeed, one might characterize language acquisition as production flowing from comprehension (KRASHEN, 1981).

In spite of the initial focus on developing comprehension skills, it would be inappropriate to suggest that this is accomplished by just talking to the students. Specific instructional techniques are used. Key vocabulary items are taught in the context of conveying real messages through the use of pictures, gestures, and other body language cues. The early emphasis is on teaching relevant vocabulary, so that when it is used in the natural flow of speech, the general content of what is being expressed can be understood.

The focus on meaning is important for pre-reading instruction as well, where ideally the child's experience and interests serve as a basis for introducing vocabulary items and sentence patterns that are subsequently presented on the blackboard or on flashcards. The usefulness of the "language experience" approach in bilingual education has been documented by PYCOCK (1977). In this study, the experimental students were introduced to reading in English by a language experience or analytic approach in grade 2. The method used in the comparison classes was a phonic or synthetic approach. Both groups of students had first begun reading in their second language, French, in grade 1. The study was undertaken to assess the relative effectiveness of the two approaches because of teachers' perceptions that the existing phonic approach to English reading instruction was confusing students who were, at grade 2, still in the process of mastering French phonics. Based on data collected at the end of grade 3, the English reading comprehension scores and linguistic analyses of English compositions showed significant differences in favour of the language experience group.

This analytic approach to reading instruction is equally valid for the students' *initial* introduction to reading in French. The oral expression of children is used as a basis for instruction: using utterances generated by and familiar to the students, global reading of corresponding sentences is introduced. Sentence recognition and comprehension of the global meaning of the sentence are emphasized, with subsequent attention directed to "analyzing" the sentence by breaking it into functional groups and learning to recognize these "second level" units. Still later, the focus moves to the syllable. The student begins to relate oral syllables to their written counterparts. Finally, the syllable is analyzed into its components; that is, the sound-symbol relationships of the language are studied.

Once students have learned how to decode written French, other aspects such as research techniques (the use of a dictionary), or literature appreciation activities, receive greater attention. Writing is introduced in the grade 1 French language arts curriculum, with typical activities including the composition of simple sentences based on vocabulary items provided by the teacher, or the completion of a short text based on reading familiar to the students.

Early immersion education has been characterized as incorporating little explicit instruction about the second language. This characterization is derived from the description of immersion as focussing on conveying *content* rather than on the *form* in which content is conveyed. However, as has already been noted, focussing on content does involve the explicit teaching of vocabulary, albeit in context and not as isolated lists of words to be memorized. Similarly, grammar is taught not as isolated rules to produce structures or patterns, but as a means of making use of words and structures to communicate more effectively. This is accomplished to some extent through the use of implicit correction by teachers during student-teacher interaction in a way similar to what occurs when native speakers interact with non-native speakers (see, for example, HATCH, 1979; KRASHEN,

1980) or adults with children (see, for example, SNOW & FERGUSON, 1977). The explicit teaching of grammar and other language rules, however, is gradually incorporated into the curriculum.

In a study of the teaching of French listening and speaking skills in elementary immersion classes, which was undertaken by IRELAND, GUNNELL & SANTERRE (1980), some language-teaching strategies and techniques used by immersion teachers were identified. The analysis was based on observations and tape-recordings of 71 visits to immersion classes from Kindergarten to grade 6 levels. The study shows that in Kindergarten and grade 1 there is very little explicit teaching of grammar, but as the children become older, the teacher's speech includes more explicit reference to, and instruction about, grammatical and structural points. From about grade 3 on, there is an increase in the time spent on grammar explanations and exercises. For the most part, grammar is dealt with in specific lessons, rather than when the lesson is focussed on teaching academic content. Thus, immersion education incorporates instruction about the second language both implicitly and explicitly.

In a study of interactions between students and teachers in primary immersion and non-immersion classrooms, RICHARDS (1978) found that the classroom climate in grade 1 and 2 total French immersion classrooms was similar to that found in regular English classrooms at the same grade levels. Further, no differences were noted in the interaction patterns in the two types of classrooms. Finally, RICHARDS (1978:223) concludes that immersion programs may have a positive influence on teaching style:

> "The encouragement of pupil initiations, use of personal experiences to enrich children's language use, and use of teaching strategies such as games and singing were all typical of the immersion teachers. These activities were participated in eagerly by the children, and seemed to contribute to a positive classroom climate."

There is little systematic information available on what actually goes on in late immersion classrooms. However, a study by CHAUDRON (1977a) focusses on the oral errors made by late immersion students and strategies used by teachers for correcting those errors. CHAUDRON analysed transcripts from several geography, history, and French language arts classes at grades 8 and 9, and found that in all cases the emphasis was on correcting content rather than form. The fact that there were grammatical errors made in student responses to questions, for example, was subordinated in the teachers' minds to the accuracy of the subject matter of the students' comments.

As a general statement, then, the immersion approach to second language education in a Canadian context involves emphasizing the communication of meaningful content material through French, rather than focussing on the teaching of the second language itself. The three immersion program alternatives described below are all based on this principle, as are other similar bilingual education programs across Canada.

Overview of Program Alternatives

Three main French immersion alternatives have been researched and evaluated by the Bilingual Education Project.

The *early total French immersion* program studied in the Carleton, Ottawa, and Toronto Boards of Education begins at the Kindergarten level where the entire (half-day) program is conducted in French. The language of instruction throughout grades 1 to 4 is also French, with the exception of a daily period of English language arts which may be introduced in grade 2 or 3. At grade 5, from 60% to 80% of the school day is still allocated to instruction in French, with the percentage of French dropping at grade 6 to between 40% and 50%. At grades 7 and 8, half the curriculum is taught in French and half in English. The secondary school follow-up programs have been designed so that the early immersion students may take three to five subject options in French at high school. The school subject areas taught in one language or the other vary among boards and even among schools, in order that the best use can be made of the teachers available. For example, if a school has a bilingual science specialist on staff at grade 6 or 7, science might be chosen as one of the subjects to be taught in French at these grade levels. If a given subject is taught in different languages in two consecutive years, it is important that the teachers and/or consultants involved discuss course content and develop the same type of sequential curriculum that characterizes any well-planned regular English program.

The evaluation of the early total French immersion programs began in 1970–71 (in Carleton and Ottawa) and 1971–72 (in Allenby Public School in Toronto). When testing ended in 1978–79, the first groups of students to enrol had reached grades 8 and 7 respectively.

Figure 2.1 depicts the early immersion program characteristics described above. It shows that the percentage of time spent in French at each grade level of this program varies slightly among boards, although the general structure of the program is similar.

The *early partial French immersion* program in Elgin County begins at the grade 1 level (following a half-day English Kindergarten) with the two

FIGURE 2.1   *Percentage of Instructional Time in French: Early Total French Immersion**

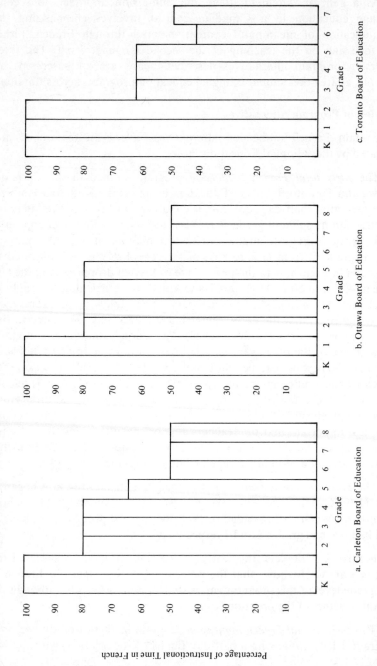

*All percentages are approximate and have been rounded to the nearest 5%. Percentages of instructional time are calculated on the basis of a 270-minute school day at grades 1–6 and a 300-minute day at grades 7–13.

FIGURE 2.2 *Percentage of Instructional Time in French: Early Partial French Immersion in Elgin County**

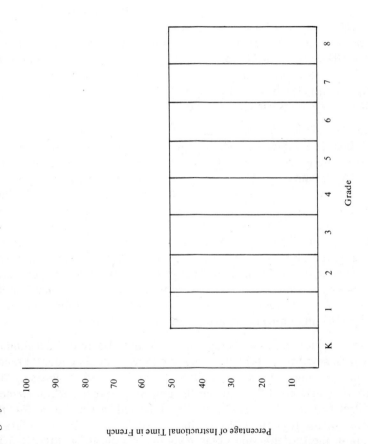

*All percentages are approximate and have been rounded to the nearest 5%. Percentages of instructional time are calculated on the basis of a 270-minute school day at grades 1–6 and a 300-minute day at grades 7–13.

languages of instruction used equally throughout the students' elementary schooling (see Figure 2.2). Since its inception in 1970–71, the partial immersion program has been limited in its intake to one class each year in only one school. Thus, although annual program evaluations were conducted until 1979, the generalizability of the Elgin County findings has always been problematic. In 1975, however, the Ottawa Roman Catholic Separate School Board established a similar partial immersion program which operates throughout the board. Since it began, that program has been evaluated annually under the direction of Dr H.P. Edwards (University of Ottawa). In Chapters 4 and 5, the Elgin County results will be supplemented by results from evaluations of the more extensive program reported on by EDWARDS, McCARREY & FU (1980). The Ottawa Separate Program differs from the Elgin County program in that it begins with a full-day Kindergarten in which 50% of the school day is devoted to instruction in French and 50% to instruction in English.

The *late French immersion* program begins at grade 8 in the Peel County Board of Education. The groups of students tested since 1970–71 began studying French in daily 20- to 30-minute periods at either grade 6 or grade 7. Approximately 55% to 70% of the grade 8 curriculum is given in French, followed in grades 9 and 10 with about 40% of the curriculum, usually history, geography, and French language arts, taught in French. At grade 11, some late immersion groups in Peel County have taken two subjects (25%) in French. For others, no school subject has been available in French at grade 11 aside from a daily class of French language arts (where post-immersion and regular English program students have, in most cases, been combined in the same class). At grades 12 and 13, the only option available in French to post-immersion students has been French language arts taught in daily French as a second language (FSL) periods.

A similar program now operates in the Toronto Board of Education (at Glenview Senior Public School) under the label "late extended" French. Although the Bilingual Education Project was involved in assessing this program only once (in 1979), the results serve as an important complement to the Peel County findings and will be discussed in Chapter 4. For the same reason, findings from the evaluation of late immersion programs operating in the Carleton and Ottawa Boards of Education (MORRISON et al., 1979) are also included wherever these are relevant.

The Toronto, Carleton, and Ottawa late immersion programs differ in some respects from each other and from the program in Peel County. The French as a second language background of the Carleton and Ottawa students, who begin core French instruction at Kindergarten, is more

FIGURE 2.3 Percentage of Instructional Time in French: Late French Immersion*

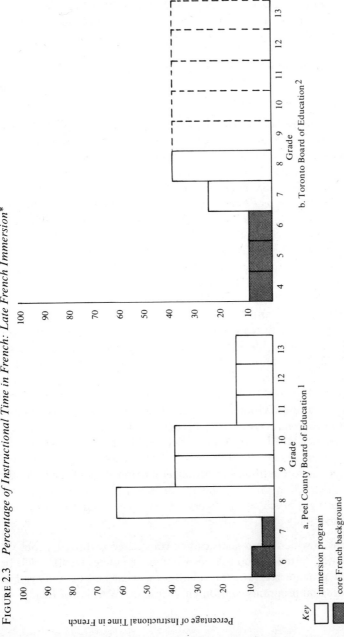

Key

□ immersion program

■ core French background

⌐ ¬ program exists at these grade levels, but has not been evaluated by the Bilingual Education Project
└ ┘

1 Only one variant of the program is illustrated.   2 Prior to entry at grade 7, students have varying exposure to core French; only one pattern is shown here.

*All percentages are approximate and have been rounded to the nearest 5%. Percentages of instructional time are calculated on the basis of a 270-minute school day at grades 1–6 and a 300-minute day at grades 7–13.

extensive than that of the Toronto students, most of whom began studying French at the grade 4 level.

The late immersion programs evaluated by the Project are depicted in Figure 2.3. The variability in the structure of the programs is more pronounced in the case of late immersion than for the early immersion programs reviewed earlier (Figure 2.1). However, for the most part, the intensive "dose" of French comes in the initial year or two years of the programs, with the amount of exposure to instruction in French remaining constant or tapering off in subsequent years.

Another useful way of describing immersion programs involves the use of numbers reflecting the accumulated hours of instructional time spent in French. In Ontario, the funding formula used for French as a second language by the Ministry of Education reflects accumulated hours of French instruction. In a document published in April 1977, *Teaching and Learning French as a Second Language*, the Ministry states that it is not the aim of all programs to make pupils fully bilingual, but that through different numbers of hours of French instruction, one of three levels of proficiency may be achieved. The levels are designated as the basic level, the middle level, and the top level. The basic level is considered to be achievable through at least 1200 hours of French instruction during the student's school career. It should enable the student to acquire a fundamental knowledge of the language, the ability to participate in simple conversation, the ability to read simple texts, and the ability to resume the study of French in later life. The middle level is considered achievable through at least 2100 hours of French instruction during the student's school career. It is expected to enable the student to read newspapers and books of personal interest with occasional help from a dictionary, to understand radio and television, to participate adequately in conversation, and to function reasonably well in a French-speaking community after a few months' residence. The top level is achievable through at least 5000 hours of French instruction during the student's school career. It should enable the student to continue his or her education using French as the language of instruction at the college or university level, to accept employment using French as the working language, and to participate easily in conversation.

The extent to which these goals can be considered realistic has not yet been empirically tested, although in Chapter 4 some results will be presented that provide relevant information on what can be achieved in each of the bilingual programs considered. (See also SWAIN, 1981b.)

The immediate use the reader can make of the accumulated hours notion is to make rapid (and somewhat superficial) comparisons among programs. Using the method of calculating accumulated hours indicated by the Ministry of Education, there are 810 instructional hours available in any one year at the grades 1-6 levels (in Ontario elementary schools), and 900 hours at grade 7 and beyond. (Kindergarten programs are generally half-day programs which yield 405 instructional hours per year.)

By the end of grade 8, students in the early total immersion programs have had the majority of their schooling in French (see Figure 2.1) and have reached, or have almost reached, the 5000-hour figure which represents the top level of proficiency as defined by the Ministry. Students in the Elgin County early partial immersion program accumulate 3300 instructional hours in French by the end of grade 8. As we have seen, the background of FSL instruction varies widely for students entering late immersion programs at grades 7 or 8 (Figure 2.3). Peel County late immersion students tested in annual evaluations have thus accumulated from 85 to 150 hours of French before entering the program, whereas Toronto late immersion students have a background varying from 90–315 hours (see Table 4.7). By the end of grade 8, therefore, Peel County late immersion students have accumulated 625 to 780 instructional hours in French, and Toronto late immersion students have had from 700 to 870 hours in French, putting them, according to the Ministry definition, still within the basic level of French proficiency.

3 Major Issues in Research and Evaluation

This chapter outlines the eight main questions asked by parents and educators about the consequences of immersion education. In the first section, the reasons for the questions, the questions themselves, and the types of "tools" used to answer them are discussed. The second section outlines the design of the research and evaluation specifically undertaken by the Bilingual Education Project. For those interested, the third section outlines and discusses some of the issues that have arisen generally in psychometric research (i.e. the measurement of observed behaviour) associated with the evaluation of educational programs. The actual results of much of the research and evaluation concerned with immersion education are considered in subsequent chapters.

Questions Frequently Asked about Immersion Education

1. *What happens to the development of students' first language (English) skills?*

When French is used as the major vehicle of communication and instruction in the classroom, it is not surprising that concern about the normal development of first language skills would be expressed, especially with respect to those skills associated with school achievement such as reading, spelling, and other aspects of written expression. For this reason, the English language skills of immersion students, especially of those in early immersion programs who learn to read and write in French before English, have been carefully monitored as the students progress through school.

Over the years and across a number of programs, a variety of techniques have been used to assess the English language skills of immersion students. Most commonly used have been the language sections of one of several commercially available standardized achievement tests such as the Metropolitan Achievement Tests, the Canadian Tests of Basic Skills, or the Peabody Picture Vocabulary Test. These tests measure such aspects of English language skills as vocabulary knowledge, reading, spelling, grammar, punctuation, and capitalization.

A standardized test is one which has been given to a large sample of students representative of those for whom the test is intended. The scores obtained become the standard, or norm, against which the performance of students taking the test at some later time can be compared. Scores from these tests are translated into grade equivalents or percentiles.

A grade equivalent refers to the performance that is expected of a student, or group of students, at a particular grade and month of their education, based on the performance of a large sample of students on whom the test was standardized. Thus, for example, if the average score in spelling of a class of grade 6 immersion students tested in April (eighth month of the sixth grade, expressed in figures as 6.8) translates into a grade equivalent of 6.10, this means that they are performing at a level that students in the tenth month (June) of their sixth grade would be expected to achieve. That is to say, their average score indicates a level of performance two months in advance of what is expected. Similarly, a grade equivalent of 6.1 would indicate a level of performance seven months behind what is expected.

A percentile refers to the percentage of the scores (obtained by students on whom the test was standardized) that fall below a certain score. Thus, if the average score in spelling of a class of grade 6 immersion students places them at the 70th percentile, this means that on the average they score better than 70% of the students on whom the test was standardized.

Techniques other than standardized achievement tests have also been used to monitor English language development. Several examples of such techniques are described below, each of which focusses on different aspects of English language proficiency. In most cases the performance of the immersion students is compared with that of students in the regular English program to determine whether the immersion students are progressing normally.

Students have been asked to write in English a short story about a picture or about one of several topics. Their written texts have been scored by teachers of the appropriate grade level on two levels: a global overall impressionistic rating and specific ratings according to such categories as spelling, sentence complexity and variety, organization, and originality (e.g. GENESEE & STANLEY, 1976). Their written texts have also been subjected to actual counts of errors in such areas as spelling, punctuation, grammar, and word usage (e.g. SWAIN, 1975a).

Similarly, students' speaking skills in English have been examined by having students retell a story that they have just heard in English. Tape-recordings of their stories have been rated on such dimensions as overall expressive ability, enunciation, rhythm, and intonation, as well as by making actual counts of grammatical errors and number of words produced (LAMBERT & TUCKER, 1972).

Students' communicative skills in English and their sensitivity to the needs of listeners have been examined by having students explain to a listener how to do something in a situation where the speaker and listener are separated by an opaque screen (GENESEE, TUCKER & LAMBERT, 1975).

Other aspects of first language development have been examined using word association tasks (e.g. LAMBERT & TUCKER, 1972). Word associa- tion tasks, in which students are given a word and told to respond to it by saying the first word that comes into their minds, are examined according to the qualitative nature of the responses.

Other techniques which have been used are oral (GRAY, 1980) and written (e.g. SWAIN, LAPKIN & BARIK, 1976) "cloze" procedures. In these tasks, students are provided with a sentence or complete text in which they must fill in missing items (words or grammatical endings on words). Completion of the task correctly or appropriately provides an indication of a student's overall intuitive feeling for the language (BERKO, 1958) and proficiency in that language (LAPKIN & SWAIN, 1977; OLLER, 1979).

In addition, parents themselves have been asked whether they think that their children's ability to read in English, or their children's English language development has suffered due to their immersion experience (e.g. McEACHERN, 1980).

2. *Do the immersion students learn more French than students in a core French program? How does their French compare to that of native speakers of French?*

Immersion programs were initiated in the belief that a more intensive exposure to French than was available in the core French program, as well as using the second language as a vehicle of communication would lead to higher levels of second language proficiency. The development of the second language skills of the immersion students has accordingly been carefully examined. In spite of the conviction that immersion education would lead to higher levels of proficiency in French than would traditional programs of French as a second language, there was a major question as to how much French immersion students would actually learn by being exposed to French in their daily classroom activities with a minimum of formal language instruction.

Although there were several tests of French for second language learners on the market at the time when immersion programs began, none was available which was specifically developed for young children who were experiencing such an intensive exposure to French, but who were not native speakers of French. Thus, in the early years of French immersion at the primary level, considerable energy was spent on developing appropriate tests and, in some cases, developing standardized norms for these tests. A description of these tests as well as some of the other techniques for examining the French language skills of immersion students follows.

Among the standardized tests of French achievement available, the one most commonly used in the evaluation of immersion programs has been the *Test de rendement en français*. The various levels of this test were standardized on a sample of native French-speaking students in Montreal. The test was originally developed by the Commission des Ecoles Catholiques de Montréal and is now distributed by the Province of Quebec. At the various grade levels, the test measures such aspects of French achievement as the identification of sounds, word knowledge (synonyms, antonyms, definitions), grammar (verb conjugations, number and gender agreement, recognition of parts of speech, use of appropriate conjunctions), spelling, and reading comprehension.

The scores of this test are translated into "stanines", which are simply another way of expressing percentiles: if, for example, a score falls within the first stanine, this means that the student is performing as well as the lowest 0%–3% of the students on whom the test was standardizsed. The percentile equivalents of each stanine are shown in Table 3.1.

Other commonly used tests, which have now been standardized, include the French Comprehension Tests (BARIK, 1975; 1976) and the *Tests de Lecture* (BARIK & SWAIN, 1979). The French Comprehension Tests are intended for Kindergarten and grade 1 immersion students and measure their understanding of spoken French words, sentences, and short stories. The *Tests de Lecture* are reading comprehension tests intended for immersion students at grade 2 to 6 levels and consist of a series of short written texts, each followed by a number of questions about the passage.

TABLE 3.1   *Percentile Ranges of Stanine Values*

Stanine	Percentile Range
9	96–100
8	89–95
7	77–88
6	60–76
5	40–59
4	23–39
3	11–22
2	4–10
1	0–3

Other commonly used tests include the *Test de compréhension auditive*, and the *Test de compréhension de l'écrit*. These tests have been developed by the Bilingual Education Project to measure listening and reading comprehension at the upper elementary and secondary school levels. In developing these tests, the purpose was to identify a number of real-life situations in which immersion students might have contact with French speakers, and to measure their understanding of the French used in each situation. Thus the *Test de compréhension auditive* consists of a number of passages recorded from radio broadcasts, such as news items, sports items, weather forecasts, advertisements, and radio drama, each followed by one or more questions to which the students respond. Similarly, the *Test de compréhension de l'écrit* consists of a number of written passages taken from various sources such as newspaper and magazine articles and advertisements, comic strips, horoscopes, television schedules, recipes, and poetic and prose literature.

Other means of examining students' performance in real-life situations have also been used. For example, students have been asked to complete a job application form and be interviewed by a prospective employer (BRUCK, LAMBERT & TUCKER, 1975). Immersion students have been paired with francophone peers and their spontaneous conversations record-ed (BRUCK, LAMBERT & TUCKER, 1974; SZAMOSI, SWAIN & LAPKIN, 1979). Also, immersion students have been interviewed by adult francophones and their language analysed (e.g. HARLEY & SWAIN, 1978a) or judged by other francophones for its acceptability (LEPICQ, 1980).

In addition, methods similar to those described above for monitoring first language development have been used to monitor second language skills. These include oral and written French cloze tests, as well as the evaluation of stories — written or told in French — on a number of dimensions.

3. *Are the immersion students able to keep up with their English-educated peers in subject content taught to them in French?*

One major concern expressed by parents and educators about immersion programs was that, because subjects such as mathematics and science would be taught in French, the students would not learn as much as if they were taught in their first language (English). Although parents wanted their children to learn French, they did not want this to happen at the expense of academic achievement. The concern was not limited to whether the students would learn as much as their English-educated peers, but also extended to whether, having acquired the knowledge through French, they would be able to transfer that knowledge for use in English contexts. Thus it was not enough to test the immersion students' achievement in, for example, mathematics and science by using tests written in the language of instruction (French). Rather the tests of subject achievement were usually given in English, even though the language of instruction about that subject was French. Needless to say, this could put the immersion students at a disadvantage, and should be kept in mind when reading Chapter 5, where the results of testing academic achievement are discussed.

For the most part, the tests which have been used to evaluate academic achievement are standardized achievement tests. Typically the tests have been given both to immersion students and to students with similar characteristics in the regular English program, and their results have been compared to determine if there are any statistically significant differences between the two groups. In addition, the scores obtained have been expressed in terms of their percentiles or grade equivalents.

The tests which have most commonly been given include the mathematics, science, and/or study skills sections of the Canadian Tests of Basic Skills or the Metropolitan Achievement Tests. Depending on the grade level being tested, the mathematics section involves subsections related to computations, mathematical concepts, and problem solving. The science section of the Metropolitan Achievement Tests consists of items related to life science, earth science, physical science, conservation, and health, and is only available for the upper elementary and secondary grade levels. From grade 3 on, the study skills section of the Canadian Tests of Basic Skills includes items related to map reading, reading graphs and tables, and knowledge and use of reference materials.

In addition, in a few instances, parents have been asked whether they think children in primary French immersion have more problems in mathematics than regular students, and whether their attendance in French immersion classes hinders the growth of general knowledge (McEACHERN, 1980).

4. *Does participation in the immersion program hinder general intellectual or cognitive growth?*

There still remains a belief among the general public that learning two languages will lead to cognitive confusion, slowing down cognitive and intellectual development. Indeed, many research findings up to the 1960s suggested that bilingual children obtained lower IQ scores than unilingual children. This research has been subjected to serious criticism, and many of the conclusions have been repudiated by the results of recent, better designed research (see SWAIN & CUMMINS, 1979, for a review). Due to this concern, however, the intellectual growth of immersion students has been monitored largely through the use of IQ tests such as Raven's Coloured Progressive Matrices, the Otis-Lennon Mental Ability Test, and the Canadian Cognitive Abilities Test.

The Progressive Matrices test is a non-verbal measure of general intelligence. In this test the child selects from an array of designs the one that is appropriate to complete a larger pattern. The non-verbal battery of the Canadian Cognitive Abilities Test is intended to measure what has been called "fluid intelligence", that is, ability that is not bound by formal school instruction. The subtests (figure analogies, figure classification, and figure synthesis) emphasise discovery of, and flexibility in, manipulating relationships expressed in figure symbols or patterns. The Otis-Lennon Mental Ability Test is an intelligence or scholastic aptitude test which measures the student's facility in reasoning and in dealing abstractly with verbal, symbolic, and figural materials, and samples a broad range of cognitive abilities (e.g. classification, analogic reasoning).

Other measures have occasionally been used to measure cognitive functioning and creativity. For example, BRUCK, LAMBERT & TUCKER (1974) used four different measures of divergent thinking:

a) Uses (e.g. Give as many uses for a shoe as you can);
b) Similarities (e.g. What are the similarities between a rug and a curtain?);
c) Lines (e.g. What could / / be?); and
d) Patterns (e.g. What could ⍵ be?).

They also used the Embedded Figures Test, in which students are asked to identify a simple form embedded in a more complex one.

5. *How do children with below average IQ fare in an immersion program?*

6. *How do children with learning disabilities fare in an immersion program?*

Parents and educators have been concerned that immersion programs may place too heavy an educational burden on students with below average intelligence, or with learning disabilities. Thus, questions 5 and 6 essentially address the same questions asked in 1, 2, and 3 (and therefore the same kinds of tests have been used to answer them), but within the context of specific characteristics of individual students.

7. *What are the social and psychological consequences of participation in immersion programs?*

This is a general question which reflects a number of more specific concerns. At one level, it concerns the possible difficulties students may have in adjusting emotionally to the immersion program. At another level, it concerns the possible outcomes of participation in immersion programs in terms of the students' social awareness and understanding of ethnic relations. These issues, and the means of examining them, are discussed in Chapter 6.

Design of Research Undertaken by the Bilingual Education Project

In its evaluation of immersion programs, the Bilingual Education Project has focussed chiefly on the first four questions outlined above. In this section, the overall design of the research carried out by the Project is described in a general way. Complete details about the basis of sample selection, the tests used, and the analyses employed in any particular year or school board can be found in the relevant annual reports (see the Appendix).

Each spring a battery of tests was administered to students in the immersion programs. In the first year of the evaluation of any particular program, the initial group of students in the program (Cohort 1) was tested. In the second year of testing, the initial group of students was tested again, as well as a new group of students who began the immersion program that year (Cohort 2). In the third year of testing, the first two groups of students were tested again, along with a new group of students who began the immersion program that year (Cohort 3). Subsequently, these three groups of students were tested each year as they proceeded through their schooling. This is illustrated in Figure 3.1 for the cohorts tested in the first five years of the early total immersion program in the Ottawa and Carleton Boards of Education.

FIGURE 3.1 *Grades and Cohorts Tested in the Annual Evaluations of the Early Total Immersion Programs During the First Five Years in the Ottawa and Carleton Boards of Education*

	Year				
Cohort	1970–71	1971–72	1972–73	1973–74	1974–75
1	K——→	1——→	2——→	3——→	4
2		K——→	1——→	2——→	3
3			K——→	1——→	2

The main reason for following three groups of students was to ensure that the initial results were not due to a "halo" effect. That is, because the first group of students were in a new program that was receiving considerable attention, it was possible that the results might be somewhat "inflated". Where results from a second and third group are similar to the first, there is reason to feel confident that the program is producing reliable or stable results. Where the results associated with follow-up groups are not similar to those of the first group, or where the conditions of the program change, it may be important to test additional follow-up groups. Thus the original research design was modified in some instances in each program evaluation. For example, in Peel County, the initial groups of late immersion students studied French as a second language in daily 20- or 30-minute periods in grade 7 before entering grade 8 immersion. Later, the program was changed so that students began taking French in grade 6. It was therefore decided to test the sixth group of students entering grade 8 immersion in order to compare their performance with that of earlier cohorts. In the case of the early immersion programs in Ottawa and Carleton, on the other hand, the program results had been so consistent in the early grades that it was decided to test only the first and third groups of students in the 1978–79 academic year.

Not all students in an immersion program were necessarily tested, nor were the test results from all students necessarily included in the data analyses. Generally speaking, where the program included a large number of students, sampling on a class basis occurred. In the elementary classes, the scores of those students who were judged by their teachers to have severe emotional problems, or who were repeating a grade, were not included in the data anlaysis. Nor were the scores obtained on French tests by students from French-speaking homes included in the analyses of the French language data.

In addition to the testing of immersion students each spring, classes of students in the regular English program at the same grade levels as the immersion classes were tested for comparison purposes. Care was taken to ensure that the students were generally comparable with respect to socio-economic status, based on information provided by personnel from each school board.

The number of students tested and included in the data analyses at each grade level in each year of testing for each program is given in Tables 3.2, 3.3, 3.4, and 3.5.

The average scores of the immersion students were compared with those of a suitable comparison group in the regular English program by means of an analysis of covariance, using IQ (and, where deemed appropriate, age) as covariates. IQ is generally positively associated with academic achievement, and if there were differences between the immersion and regular English program samples in IQ, any differences between the groups might be attributed to the differences in IQ. Although in choosing the samples, an attempt was made to ensure that the samples of students tested were similar with respect to socio-economic status (which tends to be correlated with IQ), it was impossible to preselect the samples on the basis of IQ. Therefore, analysis of covariance was used. Basically this statistical procedure makes adjustments to test scores obtained by students in relation to their measured IQ. Thus, an analysis of covariance, with IQ as the covariate, has the effect of making the groups equivalent in terms of IQ. In other words, the comparison of immersion and regular program students using covariance analysis is equivalent to preselecting the two groups on the basis of their similarity in IQ and then comparing their results on particular tests.

Results are compared statistically. A significant difference indicates that the group averages are not the same, and the level of significance indicates the confidence one has in concluding that a real difference exists. A level of significance of 0.01, for example, means that, if the experiment were repeated, in only one case in one hundred would one expect to draw a different conclusion.

TABLE 3.2   *Number of Students Included in the Data Analyses in the Evaluation of the Early Immersion Program in the Carleton and Ottawa Boards of Education*

Year	Cohort	Grade Level	Program	
			Immersion	*Regular English*
1970–71	1	K	204	151
1971–72	1	1	200	225
	2	K	275	325
1972–73	1	2	108	120
	2	1	160	170
	3	K	140	130
1973–74	1	3	173	206
	2	2	300	262
	3	1	265	250
1974–75	1	4	154	170
	2	3	263	229
	3	2	263	263
1975–76	1	5	92	117
	2	4	101	96
	3	3	110	88
1976–77	1	6	82	99
	2	5	91	104
	3	4	121	84
1977–78	1	7	90	99
	2	6	98	108
	3	5	145	69
1978–79	1	8	85	114
	3	6	184	93

TABLE 3.3 *Number of Students Included in the Data Analyses in the Evaluation of the Early Immersion Program at Allenby P.S. (later at Glenview Sr. P.S.) in the Toronto Board of Education*

Year	Cohort	Grade Level	Program Immersion	Regular English
1971–72	1	K	49	47
1972–73	1	1	30	30
	2	K	24	24
1973–74	1	2	39	49
	2	1	33	42
	3	K	40	35
1974–75	1	3	36	55
	2	2	35	50
	3	1	41	42
1975–76	1	4	34	56
	2	3	30	54
	3	2	38	47
1976–77	1	5	33	25
	2	4	24	30
	3	3	37	35
1977–78	1	6	26	25
	2	5	21	24
	3	4	33	23
1978–79	1	7	23	24
	2	6	23	37
	3	5	29	41

TABLE 3.4   *Number of Students Included in the Data Analyses in the Evaluation of the Early Partial Immersion Program in the Elgin County Board of Education*

Year	Cohort	Grade Level	Program Partial Immersion	Regular English
1971–72	2	1	—	—
1972–73	1	3	21	24
	2	2	20	24
	3	1	27	21
1973–74	1	4	23	26
	2	3	24	18
	3	2	17	20
	4	1	18	19
1974–75	1	5	18	19
	2	4	15	18
	3	3	21	18
	4	2	19	24
1975–76	1	6	18	19
	2	5	15	18
	3	4	19	18
1976–77	1	7	16	27
	2	6	10	27
	3	5	11	21
1977–78	1	8	14	—
	2	7	8	—
	3	6	8	—
	6	3	21	—
1978–79	2	8	7	—
	3	7	8	—
	6	4	22	—

TABLE 3.5 *Number of Students Included in the Data Analyses in the Evaluation of the Late Partial Immersion Program in the Peel County Board of Education*

Year	Cohort	Grade Level	Program Late Immersion	Core French
1971–72	1	8	55	54
1972–73	1	9	39	35
	2	8	54	60
1973–74	1	10	34	22
	2	9	41	30
	3	8	48	68
1974–75	1	11	30	26
	2	10	35	57
	3	9	36	30
1975–76	0	13	—	15
	1	12	19	22
	2	11	23	15
	3	10	20	15
1976–77	1	13	5	26
	2	12	8	5
	3	11	13	13
	4	10	47	45
	5	9	58	61
1977–78	2	13	6	8
	3	12	16	10
	4	11	10	—
	7	8	25	—
1978–79	4	12	14	21
	5	11	20	23
	6	10	20	24
	8	8	90	—

Some General Issues in Psychometric Research

In this section, some issues are discussed which must be faced by those undertaking the evaluation of any educational program, immersion or otherwise. The purpose of this section is to allow the reader to put psychometric research in its proper perspective, and, from this perspective, to judge the relative strengths and weaknesses of the results reported in the remaining chapters.

Psychometric research is, by definition, that which measures (quantifies) some aspect of individual performance. Thus, an overriding limitation in any psychometric study is that aspects of behaviour which are non-quantifiable, or difficult to quantify, tend not to be considered. The other side of the coin is that those aspects of behaviour that are the easiest to quantify tend to be what is examined. This is the problem underlying many of the issues associated with the evaluation of educational programs, and it pervades the discussion here in terms of (a) the students tested, (b) the nature of the tests used, and (c) the methods of analysis employed.

The students tested

An evaluation of an educational program is typically set up with the following question in mind: "How do the students in the experimental program perform relative to how they would be doing if they were not in the program: that is, if they were receiving the 'traditional' or 'usual' form of education?" Alternatively, the question may be phrased: "How do the students in the experimental program perform relative to students receiving the usual form of education, or relative to students in another type of experimental program?" In other words, research in educational evaluations typically involves the comparison of one group of students with another. However, the selection of an appropriate comparison group is often a contentious issue.

The main problem associated with the testing of students is in deciding which students to test. Educational research is rarely like "laboratory" research where the experimenter can randomly assign children to different groups — in this case, to different educational programs. Instead, the students are "assigned" on the basis of numerous factors, which often operate outside the educational system, are not always readily identifiable, are often difficult to quantify, and rarely operate randomly in distributing students into educational programs. As a result, the experimental group may have one or more characteristics (such as high motivation) which are absent in the comparison students.

What does this mean with respect to the students enrolled in French immersion programs? Because the programs are optional, this means that parents of early immersion children make the decision whether to enrol their child in the French or English program; for the late immersion students, it is ultimately the students themselves who make the decision, with a little help from their friends, parents, and teachers.

Very little is known about the characteristics of students who enter a late immersion program except that typically they have obtained above average grades in their core French course, and/or their friends have enrolled in the program, and/or their parents think it is a good idea for them to learn more French. In other words, the only readily identifiable characteristic the late immersion student brings to the program is a motivation to continue to learn French.

Similarly, very little is known about the student entering early immersion. However, a few characteristics of the parents of the early immersion children are known. For example, when asked why they enrolled their child in the program, Ottawa French immersion parents frequently indicated that it was because they wanted their child to be bilingual. They did not seem concerned about whether the program would be too difficult for their child in that they rarely mentioned it as a worry. However, many parents who enrolled their child in the English program expressed concern that the French immersion program might be an upsetting or confusing experience and that the development of basic English skills might suffer. Several parents were certain that their child would not be able to cope in the French immersion program because of special learning or personality problems (SWAIN, WESCHE & MACHIN, 1972).

In considering the question: "How do students in the immersion program perform relative to how they would be doing if they were receiving the usual form of education?" it goes without saying that the students in the immersion program, or a sample thereof, are to be tested. In order to answer this question, one needs to select a control group of students who are similar in all respects to the immersion students except that they are enrolled in the regular English program. The preceding discussion should make it apparent that it is unlikely the French immersion students and the English program students will be similar in all respects.

If *all* the characteristics of the immersion group were identifiable and quantifiable, then presumably one could select from the population of students in the regular school program those students with equivalent characteristics. But the problem is just that — the characteristics of the immersion group are not always readily identifiable nor quantifiable. For example, in the case of the primary level program, the fact that parents of the immersion children do not seem particularly concerned about their childrens' ability to cope with the immersion class may mean that the children in the program are brighter, or more extroverted, or more verbal, or simply more able to cope.

In sum, a major problem in evaluating educational programs is the selection of a control group. Typically a control group cannot be selected because: (a) the characteristics of the students in the experimental program are not always known; (b) the characteristics that are judged significant may be difficult to quantify; and (c) at least some of the characteristics may not be present among the students in the regular program.

This is a problem without a solution. However, the basic research question can be changed from "How do students in the immersion program perform relative to how they would be doing if they were receiving the usual form of education?" to "How do the students in the immersion program perform relative to students receiving the usual form of education?" Posing the question this way recognizes that students participating in the experimental program may have characteristics that differ from students not participating in the program, and that this is part of the very nature of the program. In other words, it assumes that the immersion program attracts students who, for example, in the case of late immersion students, are motivated to learn French, or, in the case of early immersion students, are more verbal, or able to cope.

In selecting such a comparison group, it is essential that every attempt be made to control variables known to affect achievement in school — for example, socio-economic status and IQ. If the immersion program is attended by children from working class families, then the comparison group should also consist of children from working class homes. In fact, when immersion programs were first implemented, they tended to serve a middle class population. At the time of the early evaluations, then, care was taken to select comparison groups from within the same school or from a school with comparable socio-economic characteristics.

Caution must be exercised in the interpretation of evaluation results when a comparison group is used. One cannot say that the bilingually educated students are doing as well as, or better or worse than they would be doing if they were being schooled in a regular English program. What one can say is that they are doing as well as, or better or worse than other students enrolled in the regular English program.

The nature of the tests used

Another question an evaluator must face is whether to use standardized tests or tests developed with the particular immersion curriculum and goals in mind. There are problems inherent in both approaches.

The development of a valid and reliable test is an extremely time-consuming process. From the construction of the first pool of test items to consultation with teachers in the program, to administration of the test, to revision of test items based on item analysis, to readministration, to final revision, to the obtaining of norms took the Bilingual Education Project a period of approximately four years. And during the period when the tests were being developed, they were also being used to measure student performance — a somewhat unsatisfactory procedure. Thus, one advantage of standardized tests is that they are readily available.

However, one problem associated with the use of standardized tests is that some items in the test may be inappropriate. For example, a number of items on achievement and IQ tests standardized in the United States include aspects of American life with which Canadian children may be unfamiliar. This problem becomes more severe the more culturally or linguistically different the group being tested is from the sample on whom the particular test was standardized.

Another problem associated with standardized tests is that they tend to maximize differences among students in a class while minimizing the differences among classes. As MACNAMARA (1974) points out, one reason for this is the choice of questions used in the test.

"Questions which deal with matters that have not been dealt with in all or nearly all classes are dropped straight away. Thus, standardized tests give little credit to the inventive or adventurous teacher or programme." (MACNAMARA, 1974: 51)

An alternative to giving standardized tests is to give tests developed with the curriculum and goals of the particular immersion program in mind. Done properly, this is a satisfactory procedure. But doing it properly is not always easy. The goals of a program rarely exist in a detailed written form. Developing a satisfactory test means getting agreement among program organizers, teachers, and consultants concerning the objectives of the program, and the appropriateness and relevancy of the test items to program goals and curriculum. Furthermore, if there are a great many classes in the program, then the problem that the standardized test developers face — that of finding the common content — is equally a problem here.

Perhaps the most serious problem with using locally developed tests is that it makes comparisons across alternative immersion programs difficult, if not impossible. For example, in the Ottawa area alone there exist several variations of the early immersion program depending on when the English Language Arts portion of the curriculum is introduced, what proportion of time is devoted to instruction in French, and the extent to which French is taught as a subject. Using a standardized test to measure French comprehension, for example, permits one to make comparisons across those variations. This is especially important when a program is being developed and variations within the same community context are being tried out, or when the same program is being tried out in different community contexts.

Because immersion programs have involved teaching a second language, their evaluations have, as we have seen, focussed largely on language-related skills. Achievement tests which measure word knowledge, spelling, punctuation, capitalization, grammar, and reading comprehension in both languages are the standard fare. These are pencil-and-paper tests which can be administered to a number of students simultaneously; they can be scored semi-automatically from answer keys or by computer. Tests which must be administered individually or which involve time and judgment in scoring (e.g. tests of creativity) are much less widely used. In other words, what is measured most frequently are those aspects of language that are easiest to measure. What is rarely measured are those aspects of language that are difficult to measure. They may be difficult to measure because they are not well enough understood for a relevant test to be developed, or because the collection and analysis of the data are simply too time-consuming.

In summary then, the problem with tests used in educational evaluations is three-fold:

a) *Type* — standardized tests permit comparisons across programs but reference to test norms is inappropriate to the extent that the groups tested differ from the norming population. Standardized tests tend not to measure learning resulting from innovative curriculum practices. Tests developed specifically to measure the outcome of specific curricular inputs, although difficult to develop, are appropriate when group comparisons are not being made. When group comparisons are made, however, the results will obviously be biased in favour of the group receiving the specific curricular input.

b) *Content* — the content measured in tests is limited. For example, standardized language tests measure the skill aspects of language rather than the communicative, creative, or aesthetic aspects.

c) *Utilization* — tests tend to be the only accepted means of obtaining performance data. Test data should be complemented by other data which may well be of a more subjective, non-quantifiable nature.

Methods of analysis

The basic research question in evaluating an immersion program typically concerns how the students in the immersion program are performing relative to students in the regular program. In addressing this question, analyses of variance and covariance, which permit the comparison of two or more groups of students on a single measure of performance, are the most commonly used methods of analysis. Analysis of covariance statistically adjusts for initial differences (e.g. in measured IQ) between the groups. Of course, the dimensions along which the groups differ initially must be identifiable and quantifiable in order to make use of these dimensions as covariates in the analysis. As already noted above, however, it may be rare that the relevant dimensions are both identifiable and quantifiable.

In and of themselves, statistical comparisons are needed since they provide critical information about differences between groups. The problems associated with the use of statistics lie in their overuse, in the information that is lost, and in their potential misinterpretation by those unfamiliar with statistics and statistical significance. Statistical significance, it must be noted, cannot be equated with educational significance. The educational significance of a statistically significant difference is a matter of interpretation by parents, educators, and researchers.

4 Linguistic Effects

In Chapter 3, reference was made to the concern of parents and educators involved in French immersion education that the English language skills of the students should develop normally in spite of their reduced exposure to English. The results of English language testing in the three bilingual programs are presented in this chapter. The question of French proficiency is then reviewed in some detail, with both quantitative and qualitative information on immersion students' second language skills and patterns of French language use.

Effects on English Language Skills

The English language, or first language, skills of early immersion students have been assessed by the Bilingual Education Project in a variety of ways. From repeated administrations of standardized tests like the Canadian Tests of Basic Skills (see Chapter 3 for test descriptions), a clear pattern of results has emerged. In Kindergarten through grade 3, immersion students lag behind their peers in the regular program in some aspects of English language skills. In grade 1, for example, immersion students' scores are lower on tests of word knowledge, word discrimination, and reading (see Table 4.1). This pattern of results persists through grades 2 and 3, where immersion students also fail to score as well as their regular program counterparts in more technical skills such as spelling, capitalization, and punctuation.

Such findings are not surprising, since no formal English language instruction is provided before grade 2, 3, or sometimes 4. By the end of grade 5, however, immersion children perform as well as, or better than, their English-educated peers on all aspects of English language skills measured by standardized tests. From grade 5 on, in those instances where there have been significant differences between immersion and comparison students, immersion groups have, with occasional isolated exceptions, outperformed their comparison groups in such areas as punctuation, spelling, vocabulary, and usage. This pattern of results is shown in Table 4.1, which presents the results for 38 separate administrations of the Canadian Tests of Basic Skills to students in Allenby Public School (Toronto Board of Education) and in the Ottawa and Carleton Boards of Education. (Details of the results of testing by the Bilingual Education Project cited in this [and other] chapters can be found in the annual evaluation reports listed in the appendix.)

The advantages in English sometimes demonstrated by early total immersion students in the middle and upper elementary grades can perhaps be explained by their knowledge of two different language systems, a knowledge which permits them to compare and contrast French and English and heightens their overall linguistic awareness (CUMMINS, 1979d; LAMBERT & TUCKER, 1972). LAMBERT & TUCKER point to "the early development of a linguistic 'detective' capacity: that is, an attentive, patient, inductive concern with words, meanings and linguistic realities" (1972:208). It seems clear from the pattern of test results that the early immersion students are able to transfer their reading skills acquired in French to their first language, they quickly become literate in English even though their exposure to formal instruction in English language arts is delayed until two or more years of schooling have passed.

The English language tests given by other researchers have also included measures of English listening and speaking skills. In the evaluations of the early total immersion program of the Protestant School Board of Greater Montreal, GENESEE (1978d) reports on tests of vocabulary, word associations, listening comprehension, and storytelling for grades 1 to 3. He finds that the immersion students' performance on the tests, which do not require literacy skills, is for the most part equivalent to that of English control groups.

Qualitative analyses of immersion children's English speech and writing have been undertaken to complement the quantitative test results just described. The Bilingual Education Project carried out a detailed analysis of errors made by immersion and comparison groups on an English "fill-in-the-blanks" (cloze) test in which no important qualitative differences were found (LAPKIN & SWAIN, 1977). Reporting on an oral storytelling task administered in grades 1 through 5 of an early total immersion program, EDWARDS & SMYTH (1976a) note few differences in the creativity of the immersion students relative to that of their peers in the regular program. Immersion children interact effectively in conversation

TABLE 4.1 *Summary of English Achievement Results for Cohorts 1, 2 and 3 in Allenby P.S., Ottawa Board of Education and Carleton Board of Education Early Total Immersion Programs*

	Cohort	GRADE 1	2	3	4	5	6	7	8
Allenby P.S.[1]	1	E word know** word discrim** reading**	E word analysis* spelling**	E spelling*	ns	ns	ns	I vocab*	
	2	E word know** word discrim** reading***	E word know* reading* total read* spelling***	E spelling*	I vocab*** reading* spelling* punct* usage* lang total**	I vocab*	I usage*		
	3	E word discrim*	E spelling***	E spelling** I vocab*** reading*** usage*	E capit*	I usage*			
OBE/CBE[2]	1	E word know*** word discrim*** reading***	ns	E spelling*	ns	I vocab** punct*** usage* lang total**	I spelling** capit*** punct*** usage** lang total***	I spelling* punct* lang total*	I spelling** lang total*
	2	E word know*** word discrim*** reading***	E word know** read* total read* spelling***	E word know** total read* spelling***	I vocab* usage* -- E -- capit*	ns	I punct* usage** lang total**		
	3	E word know** word discrim*** reading***	E spelling*	E capit*** punct* lang total**	ns	I punct** usage* lang total*	I punct* usage** lang total*		

Key: ns – no statistically significant difference between Immersion and English-taught students
 I – Immersion students' average score significantly higher than average score of English-taught students: *p ≤ 0.05; **p ≤ 0.01; ***p ≤ 0.001
 E – English-taught students' average score significantly higher than average score of Immersion students: *p ≤ 0.05; **p ≤ 0.01; ***p ≤ 0.001
[1] based on data adjusted for IQ (1978, 1979) or for age and IQ (1971–77).   [2] based on data adjusted for IQ (1979 results), or age and IQ (1971–78 results).

also: GENESEE, TUCKER & LAMBERT (1975) have reported on a study conducted in Kindergarten, and grades 1 and 2 which demonstrated that early total immersion students were more sensitive to the communication needs of listeners than were their English-educated counterparts.

Two studies of immersion students' writing ability in English have been conducted by the Bilingual Education Project. In the first study, short stories written by early total immersion and regular program students in grade 3 were subjected to a detailed linguistic analysis (SWAIN, 1975a). The analysis focussed on vocabulary knowledge, technical skills (punctuation, capitalization, and spelling), grammatical skills, and creativity as reflected in the types of stories written, the ability to write in logical chronological sequence, and the ability to write about events related to, but not depicted in, the picture that was provided to the students as a stimulus for the story. There were small differences between immersion and regular program students in all these areas (no statistical analyses were done in this descriptive study), and the immersion students' performance was seen to compare favourably. The second study of English writing ability by the Bilingual Education Project involved global assessments of compositions written by grade 5 students in both program groups. The assessments were made by teachers who did not know the students or which program they were in. These teachers found the compositions to be fully comparable. A further analysis of the variety in vocabulary use (for both nouns and verbs) and the relative length of compositions written by early total immersion and comparison students also showed no differences (LAPKIN, 1982a).

Such studies demonstrate that the English writing skills of the immersion students are similar to those of their peers in the regular program. This statement can be generalized beyond the research of the Bilingual Education Project; for example, GENESEE & STANLEY (1976) report similar findings from a study of the writing ability of both early and late immersion students. GENESEE (1974c) reports on a study of the writing skills of grade 4 immersion students. Based on teacher ratings, the immersion group lagged behind non-immersion students in spelling, but their stories were considered more original. Ratings were comparable for sentence accuracy, vocabulary choice, sentence complexity and variety, and organization. Using a more extensive measure designed to test eleven objectives of the English language arts program in New Brunswick, GROBE (undated) found that grade 5 early immersion students scored as well as, or better than, their English program counterparts.

One further indication that the English language skills of early immersion students do not suffer ill effects comes from immersion parents.

A parent survey conducted in British Columbia by McEACHERN (1980) shows that immersion parents feel that the English language skills of their children are unlikely to suffer in the program. In Ontario, a parent questionnaire distributed in the Hamilton Board of Education (1981) included a question about the students' ability to express thoughts in English: an overwhelming majority of parents (91%) indicated that they perceived no negative effects.

Turning to the partial immersion program offered in Elgin County, it might be expected that given the greater proportion of time devoted to English from the beginning of the program, there would be no tendency for partial immersion students to lag behind their English program peers in the early years of schooling. In fact, the English test results of the partial immersion students are similar to those of total immersion students: they tend to lag behind their English program counterparts until the end of grade 3 or 4. However, unlike the total immersion students who outperform comparison students in several aspects of English language skills at grade 5 or above, partial immersion students keep pace with, but do not surpass, their comparison groups.

A recent study published by EDWARDS, McCARREY & FU (1980) on the bilingual program in the Ottawa Roman Catholic Separate School Board reports on the English language skills of partial immersion students at grades 3, 4 and 5. Generally speaking, the English language results parallel those recorded for previous cohorts of total immersion students in the same board. In other words, partial immersion students perform in English as well as, or better than, their regular program peers.

In the Peel County late partial immersion study, a tendency to lag behind regular English program students in English reading comprehension was noted in the first year of the program for the first group of late immersion students only (Cohort 1, who entered the program in 1971). This deficit disappeared by the end of grade 9. Not all subsequent late immersion cohorts were tested in English in grade 9, in part because Cohorts 2 and 3 did not exhibit the same lag.

Results from evaluations of other late immersion programs are similar; for example, GENESEE, POLICH & STANLEY (1977) note no differences in English skills measured by standardized tests between late immersion and comparison students at the end of every year of the program. (This immersion program operates in the Protestant School Board of Greater Montreal; it begins in grade 7 with approximately 85% of the instructional time through the medium of French, followed by up to 40% of the curriculum available in French, at grades 8 through 11.) The writing skills of the late immersion students were also assessed at grades 7 and 11 and were found to be comparable or superior to those of regular English program students (GENESEE & STANLEY, 1976).

In summarizing the English language results from the three immersion programs reviewed, it is important to point out that although there are temporary lags in some groups (especially in early total immersion) on tests involving literacy skills, the long-term trend is for immersion groups to perform as well as, or better than, comparison groups on both standardized and non-standardized tasks. One of the challenges that lies ahead for educators and researchers is to uncover the reasons for the benefits in the area of first language development that appear to accrue to students who have spent several years in the early total immersion program.

Effects on French Language Skills

In the discussion on French language skills, the French test results associated with each of the three immersion programs will first be summarized; the programs will then be compared in terms of the second language outcomes they achieve. A third section deals with descriptive studies of the French language abilities of immersion students. This is followed by an overview of the students' own perceptions of their French language skills, and a section on the perceptions of French native-speakers about the abilities of immersion students. Finally, information on the patterns of French language use (e.g. outside school) by immersion students is provided.

Early total immersion French test results

In the initial years of the evaluations of early total immersion programs, the French skills of immersion students were most often assessed in relation to those of students in core French programs: that is, programs in which French as a second language instruction is provided in daily 20- to 40-minute periods. Since the development of listening skills is stressed in the early years, listening comprehension tests were administered from Kindergarten up to the end of grade 3. It was soon apparent that the tests were too difficult for core French students, whereas immersion students were obtaining near-perfect scores by grade 3. The French scores of the immersion students would be more usefully interpreted, it was felt, if they were considered in relation to the French language skills of native French-speaking students of the same age and grade level. This belief was reinforced by the results of administering standardized tests designed for francophone students in Quebec; even by grade 1 or 2, the immersion students were scoring as well as about one-third of native French-speaking students in Montreal, and by grade 6, as well as one-half of the Montreal comparison group.

Communicative tests of French reading and listening comprehension have also been administered at the upper elementary grade levels (grades 5 through 8). The use of such tests as the *Test de compréhension auditive* and the *Test de compréhension de l'écrit*, along with the *Test de mots à trouver* (see Chapter 3), administered to both immersion and native francophone groups, has made it possible to document the steady progress of early total immersion students to near-native levels of proficiency in several aspects of communicative French language skills by the end of grade 8. Some specific scores on two of these tests are presented in Table 4.2. The scores of the early immersion students have not been compared statistically to those of the bilingual francophone students tested in the Ottawa Roman Catholic Separate School Board (EDWARDS, COLLETTA, FU & McCARREY, 1979a). Caution must be exercised in making comparisons because of possible IQ, socio-economic, and other differences between the groups. Within these limitations, the results shown in Table 4.2 suggest that grade 8 early immersion students achieve native-like performance on the two French tests for which francophone data are available.

TABLE 4.2   *French Achievement Results of Grade 8 Early Total Immersion Students in the Ottawa and Carleton Boards of Education (Cohort 3) and of a Bilingual Francophone Comparison Group**

	Immersion	Francophone
Test de compréhension auditive, niveau B (max = 22)	15.0	14.5
Test de mots à trouver, niveau D (max = 41)	19.9	19.6

*The scores shown are group averages

One further point should be made about the French language achievement of the early total immersion students. Two alternative settings for such programs have been studied: immersion centres, where only the immersion program is housed in a given school; and dual-track schools, in which the immersion and regular English programs co-exist (LAPKIN *et al.*, 1981). It was found that the French language skills of the immersion students were enhanced by studying in immersion centres where a greater amount of French is used in the wider school environment beyond the classroom. The scores of those grade 5 immersion students studying in immersion centres were significantly higher on two French tests (listening and reading comprehension) than those of immersion students in dual-track schools. The conclusions of the study underlined the desirability of providing a school environment which includes as much French as possible (e.g. school announcements and assemblies in French).

Early partial immersion French test results

The Elgin County partial immersion students' performance on French tests has been compared both to that of core French students in other boards where core French is provided from Kindergarten on, and to that of total immersion students. In general, by grade 8, the partial immersion students tend to perform as well as total immersion students one grade level below them. Table 4.3 presents Elgin County grade 8 French scores on two tests and some comparison scores from early total immersion programs at grades 7 and 8. On the *Test de compréhension auditive*, the Elgin County results in grade 8 are similar to those of grade 7 early total immersion students in Toronto (Allenby Public School graduates who transfer to Glenview Senior School at grade 7). On both tests the partial immersion students' scores are below those of grade 8 total immersion students. As would be expected, the partial immersion students outperform core French students at any particular grade level.

TABLE 4.3 *French Achievement Results of Grade 8 Early Partial Immersion Students in Elgin County and Early Total Immersion Students in Toronto, Grade 7 (Cohort 1), and in Ottawa – Carleton, Grade 8 (Cohort 1)**

	Early Partial Immersion Elgin County, Grade 8	Early Total Immersion Toronto, Grade 7 (Cohort 1)	Early Total Immersion OBE/CBE, Grade 8 (Cohort 1)
Test de compréhension auditive, niveau B (max = 22)	13.00	13.68	14.95
Test de mots à trouver, niveau D (max = 41)	17.86	—	19.90

*The scores shown are group averages

It is useful to examine test results for the most advanced grade level (grade 5) of the partial immersion program operating in the Ottawa Roman Catholic Separate School Board (EDWARDS, McCARREY & FU, 1980). On a reading comprehension test normed on a grade 4 total immersion population across Canada, grade 5 partial immersion students scored at the 21st percentile. Elgin County grade 4 students had scored at the 23rd percentile. These results suggest that in reading comprehension, by grade 4 or 5, partial immersion students do as well as the bottom quarter of the total immersion groups (at grade 4). Edwards also reports grade 5 results for the *Test de rendement en français*, where partial immersion students score in the third stanine, as compared with total immersion students tested by EDWARDS and ourselves whose scores generally fall in the fourth, and sometimes the fifth, stanine.

Late immersion French test results

The second language skills of late immersion students have been compared both to those of their core French counterparts, and in more recent evaluations, to those of early French immersion students and francophones, where data are available. The results of French tests administered at grade 8 in Peel County (i.e. after the first year of the late immersion program) indicate that immersion students perform significantly better in all aspects of French than grade 8 core French students. Moreover, the French listening and reading comprehension scores are comparable to those of core French students who are two to three grade levels ahead of them, in grades 10 or 11 (see also SHAPSON & KAUFMAN, 1978b). In the 1979 evaluation, for example, in French reading comprehension, listening comprehension, and on a French cloze test, the immersion students' scores were significantly higher than those of core French students at grades 10, 11, and 12. This has not always been the case: in earlier annual evaluations (based on different tests of listening and reading comprehension), by grade 12, core French students had caught up in the area of reading comprehension, although not in listening comprehension. One possible explanation is that at grade 12, late immersion students have often been mixed together with core French students in the same classes; this may have had the effect of enhancing the skills of the core French students.

In recent evaluations, the results obtained by Peel County late immersion students have been considered in relation to those obtained by early French immersion students in other boards. (There is an early total immersion program in Peel County, but its students have not yet reached grade 8.) Two French tests were administered to grade 8 students in the Peel County late immersion program and in the early immersion programs of the Carleton and Ottawa Boards of Education. They were also given to the late-extended students in the Toronto Board of Education (at Glenview Senior Public School). The results for the Peel County late immersion and Toronto late-extended students, presented in Table 4.4, have been compared and their scores on the two French tests do not differ statistically. In view of the difference in accumulated instructional hours, it is not surprising that the late immersion students (in both programs) obtain scores well below those of the two early immersion comparison groups (both total and partial) on these tests.

TABLE 4.4   *French Achievement Results of Grade 8 Late Partial Immersion Students in the Peel County Board of Education (Cohort 8) and of Other Immersion Program Groups**

	Late Partial Immersion Peel County, Grade 8	Late Extended French Toronto, Grade 8	Early Partial Immersion Elgin County, Grade 8 (Cohort 1)	Early Total Immersion OBE/CBE, Grade 8 (Cohort 1)
Test de compréhension auditive, niveau B (max = 22)	8.82	10.54	13.00	14.95
Test de mots à trouver, niveau D (max = 41)	13.60	13.96	17.86	19.90

*The scores shown are group averages

These results are consistent with findings reported by the Research Centre of the Ottawa Board of Education (MORRISON *et al.*, 1979) which show that, in the Ottawa and Carleton Boards of Education, early immersion students outperform late immersion students at grade 8 in French listening comprehension, reading comprehension, general French achievement (as measured by the *Test de rendement en français*), and on a French cloze test. It is important to note that the late immersion students tested in Ottawa have had more exposure to French than the Peel County students, since in both the Carleton and Ottawa Boards of Education, core French instruction begins at Kindergarten, and students enter late immersion at either grade 6 (Ottawa) or grade 7 (Carleton). Brief program descriptions are presented in Table 4.7.

There is a high degree of similarity between the latter programs (in Ottawa) and late immersion programs in Montreal (specifically, in the Protestant School Board of Greater Montreal) evaluated by GENESEE (1979d), ADIV & MORCOS (1979), and ADIV (1980c). The most recent Montreal reports concern the relative performance of early and late immersion students at grades 10 and 11. Measures of French listening comprehension, reading comprehension, written composition, oral production, and a cloze test revealed few differences between the late immersion group who had had intensive exposure to French in grades 7 and 8 (80% +) and the early total immersion students who, in that board, are in a post-immersion follow-up program from grade 4 on, with 40% of their curriculum in French in grades 4 to 11. Among the factors which may explain the similarity in performance of early and late immersion groups from the end of grade 8 onwards, two suggested by the researchers conducting the study are particularly interesting. First, the post-immersion program of the early immersion students may be inadequate to maintain and foster further second language development beyond grade 4 (where only 40% of instructional time is provided in French). Second, the late immersion group may benefit from the more intense exposure to French (over 80% at grades 7 and 8) in their recent past.

These results from Montreal might be expected to provide a preview of possible outcomes in Ontario, once we are in a position to assess both programs towards the end of secondary school. However, in Ontario, early total immersion programs tend to maintain a higher intensity of exposure to French from grade 4 on than does the Montreal program described above (see Figure 2.1), with at least 50% of the curriculum taught in French from grades 4 to 8 (with the exception of one grade only at Allenby Public School). In other words, the Ontario and Montreal programs are sufficiently different from each other that it is not possible to predict whether comparisons of early and late immersion made in Ontario several years from now (at grade 12, for example) will yield similar results.

The issue of optimal program design is an important one. Consider, for example, the results from French testing at the secondary school level within the Peel County Board of Education presented in Table 4.5. A statistical comparison of test scores indicates that, although late immersion students make statistically significant progress from grade 8 (their first immersion year) to grade 10, no significant gains are made from grade 10 to 11, or from grade 11 to 12. This implies that the immersion follow-up program at the secondary grades, and specifically after grade 10, is adequate to maintain the students' French language skills, but not to enhance their performance in the second language.

How do the scores of secondary school late immersion students compare to those of native French-speaking students? The Bilingual Education Project was able to administer the *Test de compréhension auditive* to a bilingual francophone class in the Carleton Board of Education at grade 10 and to another class at grade 12. The results, presented in Table

4.6, indicate that the bilingual francophone students obtain scores which are well above those obtained by the late immersion students. By grade 12, then, late immersion students do not appear to have reached native-like levels of performance in listening comprehension.

TABLE 4.5 *French Achievement Results Across Grades in the Peel County Late Partial French Immersion Program**

	Grade 8 (Cohort 8)	Grade 10 (Cohort 6)	Grade 11 (Cohort 5)	Grade 12 (Cohort 4)
Test de compréhension auditive, niveau B (max = 22)	8.82	12.00	14.29	14.50
Test de mots à trouver, niveau D (max = 41)	13.60	20.37	22.00	21.89

*The scores shown are group averages

TABLE 4.6 *French Listening Comprehension Scores Obtained by Secondary School Late Partial French Immersion Students and by Bilingual Francophone Students at Grades 10 and 12**

Program	Grade 10	Grade 12
Late Partial Immersion	12.00	14.50
Bilingual Francophone	18.80	17.96

*The test used was the *Test de compréhension auditive, niveau B* (max = 22). The scores shown are group averages

One is tempted to compare the performance of the grade 8 early total and early partial immersion students with that of the grade 11 and 12 late immersion students where the accumulated hours of instructional time in French (see Chapter 2) is more comparable (although still considerably less for late immersion students). Such a comparison reveals performance that appears quite similar, indeed superior, for the late immersion students on the *Test de mots à trouver*. However, such a comparison across age levels may be invalid because of the different levels of cognitive maturity and general world knowledge possessed by the older and younger students which might affect their performance on the test independent of their linguistic proficiency.

Comparing across programs at grade 8

The programs used for comparison purposes by the Bilingual Education Project are described briefly in Table 4.7. Based on scores presented in the discussion of the three main program alternatives reviewed above (and in Tables 4.2 to 4.6), the following summary statements can be made:

a) At grade 8, early immersion students' scores on two tests administered in common are similar to scores obtained by bilingual francophone students.

b) At grade 8, the scores obtained by late immersion groups on both tests are significantly lower than those obtained by early immersion groups. The late immersion scores also appear significantly lower than those of early partial immersion students.

c) By grade 8, Elgin County partial immersion students obtain listening comprehension scores which are similar to those obtained by grade 7 early total immersion students and slightly below those of grade 8 early total immersion students. There are so few students in the partial immersion group that these statements must be considered as tentative. On the French cloze test, grade 8 partial immersion students' scores are also a little lower than those of grade 8 early immersion and bilingual francophone students.

Descriptive linguistic accounts of immersion students' second language abilities

Linguistic analysis is both time-consuming and expensive. At the same time it is rewarding, in that it provides descriptive accounts that can help define objectives for various French programs and can furnish feedback to teachers and consultants who are concerned with curriculum development and syllabus design. Several major studies have been undertaken by the Bilingual Education Project along these lines, all relating to early total immersion students.

Two of these studies have been mentioned already in the discussion of the first language abilities of immersion students. SWAIN (1975a) analyzed both English and French stories written by grade 3 immersion students. Comparing the French stories of the early immersion students to their English stories, she found the French stories to be shorter but equally varied in the use of vocabulary items (except prepositions); there were more grammatical errors and fewer "technical" errors (in punctuation and capitalization), and more spelling errors. Immersion students' stories tended to be more descriptive in French than in English. It would be interesting to compare their stories to those written by francophone peers. SWAIN concluded that more time and energy should be directed towards improving students' writing in French, since their English writing skills were developing normally.

TABLE 4.7 *French Immersion in Ontario: A Description of Some Programs to Grade 8*

Program	Board of Education	Board Terminology	Grade Program Begins	Description	Accumulated Hours of French at End of Grade 8
	Peel County	Late Partial Immersion	8	Grade 6 – core French (30 minutes daily) Grade 7 – core French (20 minutes daily) Grade 8 – 55–70% of curriculum in French	625–780
LATE IMMERSION	Toronto	Late Extended	7	Students have varying core French backgrounds prior to entering programs and have accumulated from 90–315 hours of core French instruction to end of grade 6 Grade 7 – 25–30% French Grade 8 – 40% French	700–870
	Ottawa	Late-Entry Immersion	6	K – grade 5 – core French (20 minutes daily) Grade 6 – 100% French Grade 7 – 50% French Grade 8 – 50% French	2145
	Carleton	Late-Entry Immersion	7	K – grade 6 – core French (20 minutes daily) Grade 7 – 80% French Grade 8 – 80% French	1845
EARLY PARTIAL IMMERSION	Elgin County	Early Partial Immersion	1	Grades 1 to 8 – 50% French	3330
EARLY TOTAL IMMERSION	Ottawa, Carleton	Early Immersion	K	K to grade 1 – 100% French Grades 2 to 4 – 80% French Grade 5 – 65–80% French Grades 6 to 8 – 50% French	4450–4985

In an error analysis of grade 5 early immersion responses on a French cloze test (LAPKIN & SWAIN, 1977), the comparison groups were composed of bilingual and unilingual French-speaking students at the same grade level. The immersion students made considerably more errors than the unilingual francophone students, although at least some of the errors made frequently by the early immersion students were identical to those made by the unilingual French speakers. The errors made by the immersion and bilingual francophone students were qualitatively similar, suggesting that those two bilingual groups were using similar strategies in completing the cloze passage. Once again, these comparative statements must be treated cautiously, since little information was available on the socio-economic background or IQ of the francophone groups.

Two studies of the early total immersion students' speech have been conducted. The first (HARLEY & SWAIN, 1977, 1978a) involved inter-viewing five randomly selected grade 5 immersion students, three bilingual grade 5 children of French-speaking home background attending a francophone school, and three unilingual French-speaking children from Quebec City. The interviews, which were conducted by a French-speaking adult who was not known to the children, were designed to elicit information on the verb system of the students. Among other things, the children were asked to narrate past experiences, explain current activities, and talk about the future: that is, they were expected to produce a variety of verb forms to realize specific semantic functions. The detailed linguistic analysis of the interviews shows that the verb system used by the immersion students was simplified relative to that of the six comparison students. For example, immersion students were generally unable to produce conditional forms in French in response to such questions as:

"Qu'est-ce que tu *ferais* si tu gagnais la loterie nationale?"
(= What *would you do* if you won the national lottery?)

Instead, the future might be used, thus removing the "hypothetical" nuance inherent in the conditional; or an adverb was used to convey tentativeness:

"Je *peut-être* acheter une voiture" (= I *perhaps* buy a car).

Thus immersion students are able to convey the essential message, but may use an inappropriate grammatical form to do so. The authors of the study point out that there may be little need for the immersion students to acquire a completely native-like command of French: "Once the children have reached a point in their language development where they can make themselves understood to their teacher and classmates (as they clearly have), there is no strong social incentive to develop further towards native speaker norms" (HARLEY & SWAIN, 1978a:38).

It is important to bear in mind that the only native model in an immersion classroom is the teacher and that sustained interaction with francophone peers should be encouraged if the immersion children are to attain native-like speaking abilities (SWAIN, 1978c). In another study by SZAMOSI, SWAIN & LAPKIN (1979) recordings were made of the conversations of a small sample of grade 2 immersion pupils who, on an individual basis, spent some time (once a week for two months) playing in the French-speaking homes of grade 2 pupils who were attending a francophone school. A number of the play sessions were then transcribed and analysed. The analysis was done in "functional" terms: that is, the purpose was to see how well grade 2 immersion students could use their spoken French in a natural context. It was found that the immersion students interacted with ease and naturalness and could joke, ask for clarification, issue orders, respond appropriately to the French-speaking playmate, and so on. The results of this study, along with those of the HARLEY & SWAIN (1978a) study, suggest that early immersion students can convey a rich range of meanings in French, but that their way of doing so remains non-native.

The linguistic outcomes of early partial and late immersion programs have received less descriptive research attention. In one study, however, MORRISON *et al.* (1979) compared grade 8 early total and late partial immersion French compositions and found that the early immersion students wrote longer sentences with fewer errors, although the average length of the compositions was similar for the two groups.

In an interview study conducted in Peel County at the grade 12 level, the conversational French skills of late immersion students were compared to those of core French students (SWAIN & LAPKIN, 1977). The interview data suggest that the late immersion students were better able to cope with the communicative demands of conversing in French.

Students' perceptions of their French language abilities

A Second Language Student Survey was administered to early total and late immersion students in the 1979 annual evaluations conducted by the Bilingual Education Project. Four questions of the Survey were grouped together (under one factor) because they related to the students' self-assessment of their skills. Students were asked how well they felt they could understand French TV programs and newspapers or magazines; they were also asked how well they could make themselves understood in a conversation with a stranger, and they were requested to assess the extent of their willingness to engage in French conversation outside the school context. A second relevant factor, grouping five related questions, dealt with the students' expressed preferences vis-à-vis their French program; for example, would they prefer to spend more, or less, or the same amount of time learning in French at school? On both factors, the early immersion students scored higher: they considered themselves more skilled in French than did the late immersion students, and they preferred to have more French in their school program.

In the St. Lambert study (LAMBERT & TUCKER, 1972) the views of early total immersion students in grades 4 and 5 were contrasted with those of students in the regular English program taking core French. At both grade levels, a large percentage of early immersion students (from 36% to 70%, depending on the skill area) felt that they spoke, understood, read and wrote French as well as they did English. A second study (GENESEE, 1978f) documented the views of grade 6 early and grade 11 late immersion students in the Protestant School Board of Greater Montreal on their program and their self-assessment of their French skills. The self-reports of all the immersion students corresponded to trends already noticeable in their test results, with both groups rating their listening comprehension skills as their strongest second language ability and their oral production skills their weakest. Both groups of immersion students were well satisfied with their programs; no differences were apparent between early and late immersion students.

Native speakers' perceptions of immersion students' French language skills

One of the undisputed objectives of immersion programs is that its students be able to communicate effectively in French with native French speakers. LEPICQ (1980) conducted the first empirical study of the acceptability of immersion students' speech to bilingual and unilingual French peers and adults. The study involved presenting recorded speech samples from interviews with eight grade 6 Ontario immersion students and four unilingual French-speaking Quebec students to a group of judges. The researcher interviewed the 96 judges (bilingual and unilingual, children and adults), to elicit views on the acceptability of the speech samples. The judges tended to apply different criteria in evaluating the immersion and francophone comparison students, demonstrating that their expectations were different for the two groups. In general, the immersion students were assessed favourably, and LEPICQ (1980:592) suggests that early immersion programs

"constituent une préparation tout à fait adéquate à la communication éventuelle entre les apprenants et les francophones de naissance" (= provide a completely adequate preparation for potential communication with native French speakers in the future).

Immersion students' patterns of French language use

A number of questions on the Second Language Student Survey used in the evaluations of the Bilingual Education Project have been related to three important factors in developing French proficiency: the students' self-motivated use of French, their opportunity to use French, and the use of French in the home. In considering the first of these, it is noteworthy that the students (even those living in a bilingual milieu) report very little self-initiated use of the language (e.g. reading French magazines or newspapers, listening to French radio, watching French television, using French on vacations). This lack of self-initiated language use seems to characterize findings from similar questionnaires used in other evaluations. In a study already referred to, GENESEE (1978f:38) reports:

> ". . . it does not seem that they [immersion students] are more active in initiating conversations in French or in actively seeking out situations where French could be used . . . there was no evidence that they use French more outside school than do their peers in the regular program."

As one illustration of this tendency not to seek out opportunities for using French, immersion and non-immersion students alike indicated minimal use of French media (including television, radio, cinema, books, magazines, and newspapers). At both grades 6 and 11, however, immersion students indicated that they were more likely than comparison students in the regular program to respond in French if spoken to in French. This pattern of questionnaire responses suggests a distinction between "active" and "reactive" language use, with active referring to self-initiated use of French (e.g. choosing French television programs to watch), and reactive referring to French language use initiated by others (e.g. in interpersonal communication). GENESEE (1980b:20) concludes

> "that the favourable attitudes of the immersion children and their parents along with their superior second language competence were sufficient to engage them in reactive language use but not in active language use".

What about the immersion students' opportunity to use French? Here there is a significant difference between the early and late immersion students tested by the Bilingual Education Project (LAPKIN *et al.*, 1982).

The early immersion students report more opportunities to use French outside of school than do late immersion students. In school, the early immersion students report that they use French in class with their teacher almost all the time, differing significantly from the late immersion students who report using French with their teacher about half the time.

Learning French and IQ

Is there a relationship between academic ability as measured by standardized IQ tests and the ability to learn French in an immersion context? In summarizing several relevant studies of early immersion students (from Kindergarten through grade 9), GENESEE (1976c) states that the acquisition of literacy skills (reading and writing) in French is associated with the students' IQ level, while the acquisition of interpersonal communication skills (listening and speaking) is not. Furthermore, he specifies that

> "Below average students in total early immersion acquire functional competence in speaking and understanding French to the same extent as average and above average students in the program" (p.23).

In discussing children with specific learning disabilities, behaviour problems, and other difficulties, BRUCK (1979b) concludes that such students progress as well in an early immersion program as they would in a regular English program and that the immersion program provides "a particularly appropriate environment for many 'slow learners' or 'learning disabled children' to learn French" (p.46). These same children tend not to learn French in traditional core French programs.

Summary of French Language Findings

The receptive skills (French listening and reading comprehension) of the French immersion students appear to develop to near native-like levels by grade 8 of an early total immersion program. French speaking and writing skills, however, remain less native-like, although immersion students are able to convey the meaning of what they want to say. Based on results from a listening comprehension test, there is some indication that early total immersion students' performance (at grade 8) is closer to that of bilingual francophone peers than is the performance of late immersion students (at grade 12). In addition, the Ontario results show that the performance of grade 8 early immersion students in all skill areas tested is superior to that of late immersion students in grade 8 who have had one, two, or three years of exposure to French in late French immersion programs.

It is important that comparisons of the second language outcomes of early and late immersion programs continue to be carried out at higher grade levels (e.g. in two years' time, when both groups have reached grade 12 in Ontario), and that improved measures of the productive skills (especially speaking) be developed and used to describe the French language proficiency of different immersion groups at that advanced stage. Similarly, it is important to make systematic comparisons with the French language skills of francophones, since attaining a similar degree of French proficiency constitutes a desirable objective for immersion programs.

Immersion students have a high level of confidence about their own second language abilities, and recognize that their speaking skills are the weakest area. Nonetheless, native French speakers assess immersion students' speech favourably. If immersion students can be encouraged to actively use French language outside of school, and if educators can be persuaded to provide as intensive an exposure as possible to French in school in post-immersion follow-up programs, the second language skills of immersion students in all programs can be expected to be even better.

5 Academic Outcomes of Immersion Education

As indicated in Chapter 3, one of the major concerns of parents and educators about immersion education was whether immersion students would be able to keep up with their English-educated peers in subject content taught to them in French. Associated in part with this concern was the more general question of whether a child's intellectual growth might be impeded as a result of attempting to process information in more than one language. A further worry was that the immersion students might develop poor work-study habits because of restlessness and inattentiveness that could result if the students were not able to understand what was being said to them. These issues are the focus of the present chapter.

A considerable amount of information has been gathered in Ontario and elsewhere in Canada addressing these issues. For example, virtually every evaluation undertaken of an immersion program has measured the students' achievement in mathematics, comparing the immersion results against national norms, or against similar students studying mathematics in English in the same school or school board. Perhaps what is most remarkable about the findings on these issues is the consistency of what the data reveal. The data collected in the context of the Bilingual Education Project and discussed in the following pages, therefore, serve to illustrate the results now widely confirmed for immersion programs across Canada.

In this chapter, a section on early total immersion programs is followed by sections on early partial immersion programs and late immersion programs. The definition and description of each program are found in Chapter 2. The results of the Bilingual Education Project which are summarized in this chapter are drawn from the annual reports listed in the appendix.

Early Total Immersion

Students in early total immersion programs are initially taught all content material in French. At later grade levels when the proportion of the curriculum taught in English is increased, some subjects are taught in English. The choice of subjects taught in English or French has tended to be made on the basis of available teaching expertise and other administrative constraints within a school. When a choice unconfined by administrative constraints can be made among subjects to be taught in French, at least two factors need to be kept in mind: (a) the extent to which student achievement in the subject area may depend on language of instruction, and (b) the usefulness of the subject content in advancing French language proficiency. A subject which allows considerable opportunity for students to hear and use the second language in rich and creative ways seems most appropriate.

In the early years of schooling, the primary focus of the curriculum is on language arts and mathematics. Standardized tests are readily available for measuring achievement in these subjects. At later grade levels when science becomes another major focus of the curriculum, this is reflected in standardized achievement tests as well. For other subjects such as social studies (history and geography) where the sequencing of content, as well as the content itself, is more flexible, locally developed achievement tests based on school board curricula are more appropriate. Because arithmetic/mathematics is always taught in French in the primary grades of total immersion, and because standardized tests (in English and French) are available to measure achievement in this subject, the most extensive information is available about achievement in mathematics when it is taught through the medium of the second language.

The research available on subject matter achievement has addressed two questions:

1) Are immersion students able to keep up with their English-educated peer group in subjects taught to them in French?
2) Are achievement scores affected by the language of the test?

The first question has been approached within the context of the Bilingual Education Project by testing the mathematics and science achievement of immersion and English-program students in the same school or school board. The mathematics and science tests were given in English, even though immersion students had been taught these subjects in French. The results for mathematics are shown in Table 5.1 and for science in Table 5.2.

TABLE 5.1 *Summary of Mathematics Achievement Results for Cohorts 1, 2 and 3 in Allenby P.S., Ottawa Board of Education and Carleton Board of Education Early Total Immersion Programs*

| | Cohort | GRADE | | | | | | | |
		1	2	3	4	5	6	7	8
Allenby P.S.[1]	1	ns	ns	ns	ns	ns	ns	E concepts*	
	2	ns	ns	ns	I concepts** prob solving* math total**	I concepts* prob solving** math total**	ns		
	3	I arith total**	ns	I concepts*** prob solving** math total***					
OBE/CBE[2]	1	ns	ns	E prob solving*	ns	ns	ns	ns	ns
	2	ns	ns	E concepts* prob solving*	ns	ns	ns		
	3	I computation***	ns	ns	ns	I prob solving*	ns		

Key:

ns – no statistically significant difference between Immersion and English-taught students

I – Immersion students' average score significantly higher than average score of English-taught students: *$p \leq 0.05$; **$p \leq 0.01$; ***$p \leq 0.001$

E – English-taught students' average score significantly higher than average score of Immersion students: *$p \leq 0.05$; **$p \leq 0.01$; ***$p \leq 0.001$

1 based on data adjusted for IQ (1978, 1979) or for age and IQ (1971–77)

2 based on data adjusted for IQ (1979 results), or age and IQ (1971–78 results)

TABLE 5.2 *Summary of Science Achievement Results for Cohorts 1, 2 and 3 in Allenby P.S., Ottawa Board of Education and Carleton Board of Education Early Total Immersion Programs*

		GRADE			
	Cohort	5	6	7	8
Allenby P.S.[1]	1	ns	I**	ns	
	2	ns	ns		
	3	ns			
OBE/CBE[2]	1	ns	ns	ns	ns
	2	ns	ns		
	3	ns	ns		

Key:
ns – no statistically significant difference between Immersion and English-taught students
I – Immersion students' average score significantly higher than average score of English-taught students: *p $\leq$ 0.05; **p $\leq$ 0.01; ***p $\leq$ 0.001
E – English-taught students' average score significantly higher than average scores of Immersion students: *p $\leq$ 0.01; **p $\leq$ 0.01; ***p $\leq$ 0.001
[1] based on data adjusted for IQ (1978, 1979) or for age and IQ (1971–77)
[2] based on data adjusted for IQ (1979 results), or for age and IQ (1971–78 results)

Table 5.1 gives the results for 38 separate administrations of standardized mathematics achievement tests to students in Allenby Public School in Toronto and in the Ottawa and Carleton Boards of Education in Ottawa. (The numbers of students tested for each cohort and grade level are given in Table 3.2.) In the majority of comparisons between immersion students and their English-educated peers, their average scores are equivalent: that is, there are no statistically significant differences between the groups on the test as a whole, or on any of the subtests dealing with mathematics concepts or problem solving. In three instances, an English-taught group scored significantly higher than an immersion group on one or two of the subtests, but never on the test as a whole. However, in six instances, an immersion group scored significantly higher than its comparison group on one or two of the subtests. Additionally, in four of these cases, the immersion students demonstrated superior performance on the mathematics test as a whole. The overall picture emerging from these comparisons is that immersion students are able to keep up in mathematics with English-educated students of similar IQ level and socio-economic background. They are able to learn mathematics in French and transfer the knowledge acquired in a French context to an English one. There is no indication over the long run of any detrimental effects resulting from being taught mathematics in French.

Similar conclusions are evident from the evaluations of other early total immersion programs (e.g. CITY OF HAMILTON BOARD OF EDUCA-TION, 1979; EDWARDS & SMYTH, 1976a; EDWARDS, COLLETTA, FU & McCARREY, 1979a; GENESEE, 1978d; GRAY, 1980; LAMBERT & TUCKER, 1972; WOLSK, 1977).

The conclusions with respect to science achievement in the early total immersion program are similar. The results from the Bilingual Education Project's study are shown in Table 5.2, where it can be seen that the average scores of the immersion students and their English-taught peers are equivalent in 14 separate administrations of standardized science achieve-ment tests from grades 5 to 8. One exception occurs in grade 6 where the immersion students outperformed their English-educated comparison group. These findings are similar to other studies which have examined science achievement (e.g. BRUCK, LAMBERT & TUCKER, 1976a; EDWARDS, COLLETTA, FU & McCARREY, 1979a), indicating that science achievement is neither positively nor negatively affected by instruction in the second language.

The comparison of students across programs within a school or school board reflects only the relative standing of each group. It does not indicate the actual scores obtained by the immersion students. The data collected by the Bilingual Education Project show that the immersion students typically score above their expected grade equivalents. Table 5.3 illustrates this in mathematics achievement in grades 3 to 6 (Cohort 2). Although the absolute figures from other early total immersion programs are in some cases higher and in some cases lower, they are usually at least at the expected grade equivalence, and reflect the general socio-economic and IQ characteristics of the students participating in the immersion program.

TABLE 5.3   *Grade Equivalents[1] in Mathematics for Grades 3-6 of Cohort 2 in Allenby P.S., Ottawa Board of Education and Carleton Board of Education Early Total Immersion Programs*

Expected Grade Equivalent	Actual Grade Equivalent	
	Allenby P.S.	*OBE / CBE*
3.8	4.0	4.2
4.8	5.3	5.1
5.8	6.4	6.0
6.8	7.7	7.0

[1] Based on scores unadjusted for IQ

Although absolute figures are interesting, the important point here is whether immersion students are doing as well in science and mathematics as their peers in the English program. By comparing the immersion students taking mathematics or science in French to students with similar characteristics but taught in English (and statistically controlling for differences in IQ — see Chapter 3), the answer which clearly emerges from these results, and those of other studies, is that early total immersion students are achieving as well as their peers studying mathematics or science in English.

Other evidence which supports the conclusion that early immersion students are able to keep up with their English-educated peers in subjects taught to them in French comes from the Ottawa Roman Catholic Separate School Board (EDWARDS, DOUTRIAUX, FU & McCARREY, 1977). Geography and history tests were developed based on the grade 7 curriculum of the board. The tests were administered in English to grade 7 early immersion students studying history and geography in French and to grade 7 students studying these subjects in English. There were no differences between the two groups on either of the tests. When immersion parents were asked if they thought French immersion hindered their children's growth in general knowledge, more than 90% said that it did not (McEACHERN, 1980). Thus, from the evidence available, it would appear that early total immersion students are able to study history, geography, science, and mathematics in French and still maintain achievement levels consistent with students studying the same subjects in English.

The second question raised concerned the effect that the language of the test might have on achievement scores. This is a particularly crucial issue in settings where students might be required to take tests in their second language. Students who come from non-English homes but attend English schools are constantly faced with this situation. If they demonstrate inferior performance, is it because they do not possess the content knowledge required to perform satisfactorily on the test, or is it because they are weak in the language of the test? In the case of immersion students, we know from testing their knowledge about science and mathematics in English that they have achieved satisfactory levels of performance. But what if they were tested in French? There is relatively little information related to this question, but there are two sets of relevant data: one pertains to achievement in social studies, the other to achievement in mathematics.

With respect to achievement in social studies, French and English tests, which were designed specifically to correspond to the grade 4 social studies curriculum in the Ottawa Roman Catholic Separate School Board, were administered to grade 4 students studying social studies in French in two different programs: a total immersion program and a 60-minute-a-day (extended-core) program. Results from the English versions of the test revealed no differences in social studies achievement between the groups. Results from the French versions of the test, however, revealed a highly significant difference in favour of the immersion students. Furthermore, the immersion group performed in French as they had in English, whereas the extended program students' score when tested in French was much lower than when tested in English, even though they had been taught social studies in French. These results suggest that testing students in a second language in which they are not highly proficient may not accurately reflect their level of knowledge and skills related to the content of the test.

The second set of relevant data is related to achievement in mathematics. In the initial years of the Bilingual Education Project, the students in grades 1 and 2 were administered a standardized test of mathematics in French, the *Test de rendement en mathématiques*. It contained items involving elementary set theory, equations, and the oral presentation of short problems. Half of the immersion students took the test in French, while the other half took a translated version in English. Comparison groups of English-educated students also took the test in English. The results of the three groups were compared at each grade level, and no differences were found among the groups.

Both the above examples — of achievement in social studies and mathematics — suggest that total immersion children have mastered enough French to permit an accurate reflection of their competence in mathematics and social studies to manifest itself. At the same time, the results in social studies suggest that testing in the second language is a risk if one wishes accurately to measure achievement in content knowledge and skills.

Overall, the results of the achievement testing in early total immersion programs imply in a general way that the students' intellectual development has not been affected negatively by their bilingual experience. Another indication is that IQ scores obtained annually show no sign of decreasing over time. Indeed, if one looks at changes in IQ scores over time, one finds a general trend in which the IQ scores of immersion students increase more than those of English-program students (BARIK & SWAIN, 1976f), suggesting possible beneficial effects of the bilingual experience on cognitive development. EDWARDS, DOUTRIAUX, McCARREY & FU (1976) studied the creativity scores of grade 5 and 6 early immersion students in contrast to those of English-program students, and found that grade 5 early immersion students had higher verbal creativity scores and that grade 6 early immersion students had higher verbal and non-verbal creativity scores. BRUCK, LAMBERT & TUCKER (1974) found that on measures of cognitive flexibility and divergent thinking, when differences between immersion and English-educated students occurred, they consistently favoured the immersion students. There is, therefore, no evidence to suggest that the bilingual education experienced by immersion students has led to any negative consequence with respect to general intellectual functioning. (See also SWAIN & CUMMINS, 1979.)

It is interesting to note as well that there is a trend for the immersion students in the Bilingual Education Project study to have better work-study skills (reading of maps, graphs, and tables, and knowledge and use of reference material) than the comparison groups. As Table 5.4 indicates, of the 22 separate administrations of the work-study skills section of the Canadian Tests of Basic Skills from grades 3 to 8, the immersion students perform significantly better than their English-educated peers in just over half the testing sessions.

In sum, students in the early total immersion program are able to master the content of such subjects as mathematics, history, geography, and science to the extent that their peers in the regular program have. Furthermore, the total immersion experience seems to have sharpened their work-study skills and has left them with no sign of cognitive confusion. Indeed, the results suggest that the immersion students may be reaping positive benefits, not only in enhanced English language skills, as was indicated in Chapter 4, but also in more specific intellectual skills.

Early Partial Immersion

The information available for early partial immersion programs is much more limited than it is for early total immersion programs, in part because there have been fewer such programs. In Ontario, there are two well-established early partial immersion programs: one in Elgin County involving a relatively small number of students (see Table 3.4) and one in the Ottawa Roman Catholic Separate School Board involving almost all the students in the Board. Unfortunately, the mathematics achievement data available for the Ottawa program are not useful in answering the question of whether the immersion students are able to keep up to English-taught students because mathematics has been taught in English. Science achievement has not been tested in the Ottawa program. Thus, no cross-program comparisons are possible with respect to achievement data. A third partial immersion program, which was established in Edmonton in 1974, has also been evaluated (EDMONTON PUBLIC SCHOOLS, 1980), and provides

TABLE 5.4 *Summary of Work Study Skills Results for Cohorts 1, 2 and 3 in Allenby P.S., Ottawa Board of Education and Carleton Board of Education Early Total Immersion Programs*

		GRADE					
	Cohort	3	4	5	6	7	8
Allenby P.S.[1]	1				ns	I map reading* ref materials*	
	2	ns	I map reading* graphs/tables*** ref materials*** work study skills total*	I graphs/tables** ref materials*** work study skills total***	graphs/tables*		
	3	I map reading** graphs/tables** ref materials*** work study skills total***	I map reading** ref materials*** work study skills total*	ns			
OBE/CBE[2]	1			ns	ns	ns	ns
	2		I Map reading* graphs/tables* work study skills total*	ns	I ref materials**		
	3	ns	ns	I graphs/tables* ref materials*** work study skills total**	I ref materials*		

Key:

ns – no statistically significant difference between Immersion and English-taught students

I – Immersion students' average score significantly higher than average score of English-taught students: *p ≤ 0.05; **p ≤ 0.01; ***p ≤ 0.001

E – English-taught students' average score significantly higher than average score of Immersion students: *p ≤ 0.05; **p ≤ 0.01; ***p ≤ 0.001

[1] based on data adjusted for IQ (1978, 1979) or for age and IQ (1971–77)

[2] based on data adjusted for IQ (1979 results), or age and IQ (1971–78)

some useful comparative information on the mathematics achievement of students in early partial immersion programs.

Table 5.5 presents the mathematics achievement results from Elgin County. The results indicate either that there are no differences between the partial immersion students and their respective English-educated comparison groups, or that the partial immersion students do not do as well on some of the subtests and/or the mathematics test as a whole. In no case does a partial immersion group outperform its comparison group. The EDMONTON PUBLIC SCHOOLS' (1980) results also show inferior performance on the part of partial immersion students in grades 3 and 4, but not grade 5. These results suggest that partial immersion students may be at some disadvantage in acquiring mathematical skills and knowledge in French. It has been suggested (SWAIN, 1978a) that this is because their French skills, which at these grade levels are not on a par with those of early total immersion students (see Chapter 4), may be insufficient to deal with the more complex aspects of the subject matter they are being taught in these grades.

What happens if the partial immersion students are taught mathematics in English after being taught it in French? This, in fact, was done in the 1977–78 academic year in Elgin County, so that grades 5, 6 and 7 (Cohorts 3, 2, and 1 respectively) were taught mathematics in English. The results are ambiguous: the grade 7 partial immersion group's performance improved relative to its comparison group, whereas the reverse was the case for the grade 5 partial immersion group. There was no difference in grade 6 performance (Table 5.5).

The science achievement data (Table 5.5), also indicate either no differences between the partial immersion students and their respective comparison groups, or inferior performance on the part of partial immersion students. The general trend indicated by the information currently available is that early partial immersion students may experience more difficulty in maintaining standards in subjects taught to them in French commensurate with those of their English-educated peers. On the other hand, no such difficulties are encountered by early total immersion students. Furthermore, in terms of work-study skills, early partial immersion students show no advantage over their respective comparison groups (see Table 5.5) as was the case for early total immersion students. The IQ scores of the Elgin County immersion students were initially high, and remained high throughout the years of testing. This suggests, as with total immersion students, that the bilingual education experience did not result in negative consequences with respect to general intellectual functioning.

TABLE 5.5 *Summary of Mathematics and Science Achievement and Work Study Skills Results for Cohorts 1, 2 and 3 in Elgin County Board of Education Early Partial Immersion Program*[1]

	Cohort	1	2	3	4	5	6	7
					GRADE			
MATHEMATICS	1						E concepts*** math total*	ns
	2		ns	ns	E computation *** math total**	ns	ns	
	3	ns	ns	E computations*** concepts*** prob solving** math total***	ns	E concepts*		
SCIENCE	1						E**	ns
	2					ns	ns	
	3					E*		
WORK STUDY SKILLS	1						ns	ns
	2				ns	ns	ns	
	3					ns		

Key:

ns – no statistically significant difference between Immersion and English-taught students

I – Immersion students' average score significantly higher than average score of English-taught students: *p ≤ 0.05; **p ≤ 0.01; ***p ≤ 0.001

E – English-taught students' average score significantly higher than average score of Immersion students: *p ≤ 0.05; **p ≤ 0.01; ***p ≤ 0.001

[shaded] taught in English

1 based on data adjusted for age and IQ

Late Immersion

In the Peel County late immersion program, mathematics, science, history, and geography were taught in French in grade 8. In later grades, only history and geography were taught in French. Achievement in all these subjects has been assessed in grades 8, 9, and 10.

The initial grade 8 late immersion group was given a standardized science test at the beginning and end of grade 8. They did as well as their comparison group at the beginning of the grade 8 year but not at the end of the year. This finding was interpreted as revealing a slight negative effect of the late immersion program on general science concepts attainment. In the following years, however, when the late immersion students were taught science in English, their performance was equivalent to that of students who had not taken science in French in the grade 8 year.

Mathematics achievement has also been assessed with inconsistent results. Of the three cohorts of late immersion students followed by the Bilingual Education Project in Peel County (see Table 3.5), one grade 8 group's performance was equivalent to that of its English-instructed group, a second group scored better than its comparison group, and a third group did not perform as well as its comparison group. When taught mathematics in English the following year, the first group demonstrated an achievement level equivalent to that of its comparison group, the second maintained its superior performance, and the third group was not retested.

In studies of other late immersion programs where mathematics has continued to be taught in French, the results indicate that the immersion students do as well in mathematics as their English-instructed comparison groups (e.g. EDWARDS, McLAUGHLIN, McCARREY & FU, 1978; MacDONALD, 1980) or in some cases better, or worse, than students studying mathematics in English (e.g. WIGHTMAN, 1977). Wightman suggests that, based on comparisons across immersion classes, factors other than the immersion experience may be influencing the mathematics score.

History and geography achievement in late immersion programs has also been measured. In Peel County, late immersion students took locally developed tests based on the high school history and geography curriculum three times a year. Their average scores in grades 9 and 10 ranged from 70% to 80%. These figures are not directly comparable to those of students taught history and geography in English, as the latter were given different tests. However, the scores obtained by the late immersion students in history and geography were consistent with their own scores in other subjects and with scores obtained by their comparison groups when tested in English. EDWARDS, DOUTRIAUX, McCARREY & FU (1977) found that on locally developed tests, late immersion students in grade 7 (their initial year) demonstrated equivalent levels of achievement in history and geography as students studying these subjects in English. HENDELMAN (1975) reports similar results for late immersion students in the Ottawa Board of Education.

Results from Montreal reveal that, for those late immersion students who have continued to take several course options in French throughout secondary school, the average scores they obtained on Ministry of Education Leaving Examinations taken in French are higher than those obtained by francophones in the rest of Quebec. These examinations include *histoire, géographie,* and *mathématiques* (GENESEE, 1976d).

Overall, the results pertaining to the academic achievement of late immersion students are somewhat inconsistent. In some cases, late immersion students do not perform as well on tests of subject achievement taught in French and tested in English as do their English-instructed counterparts. The results appear to be related to the subject and to the amount of prior core French instruction that the students have had. Where late immersion students have had core French instruction each year from grade 1 to the immersion year, as in Montreal and Ottawa, the level of mastery of content taught in French appears to be comparable to that attained by English-instructed students (GENESEE, POLICH & STANLEY, 1977; STERN *et al.,* 1976b). If the amount of prior core French instruction is more limited, however, poorer performance in some subject areas (e.g. science) has been noted. As was suggested for early partial immersion students, this may be because their second language skills are not sufficient to cope satisfactorily with the complex subject matter being taught to them in French.

Conclusions

The information presented in this chapter suggests that in general and over the long run, immersion students are able to maintain standards of achievement consistent with those of their English-educated peers. This is not always the case, however, on a short-run basis. In particular, students in early partial or late immersion programs, whose second language skills may initially be insufficient to deal with the complexities of the subject material taught to them in French, may have some academic difficulties. The work-study skills of immersion students have not suffered. Indeed, the information available suggests that they may be enhanced in the early total immersion environment. Furthermore, there is no evidence to suggest that an early exposure to bilingual schooling results in cognitive confusion.

Rather, normal intellectual growth occurs, with some indication that growth may be enhanced in an early total immersion setting.

The fact that academic achievement can be maintained at expected levels when the subject is taught in French leaves open the choice of subjects to be taught in that language. A subject which allows students many opportunities to hear and use the second language in creative ways and with context-rich topics seems to us most appropriate.

6 Social and Psychological Aspects of Immersion Education

Most of the research associated with immersion education has been concerned with its academic and linguistic consequences. Little attention has been paid to the social and psychological aspects of immersion education. Some notable exceptions in the research carried out in Ontario and Quebec will be considered in this chapter.

There are two main facets to the issue of social and psychological aspects of immersion education. First, there is the question of the children's adjustment to the program, especially the adjustment of young children to the early total immersion program. It was felt by some parents and educators that beginning school coupled with not being able to understand the teacher, might create problems. Their concern was fed by a mistaken belief that the children would be denied the possibility of spontaneously expressing their feelings and ideas because they would not be allowed to speak English. This, as we have already seen, is not what occurs in an early immersion program. True, the teachers speak only French, but they understand English, and for much of the first year the children talk to each other and their teachers in English. The children are certainly not inhibited from expressing themselves in their mother tongue. Second, there is the question of the impact of immersion programs on students' feelings — feelings towards themselves and speakers of the target language, as well as their feelings about the wider socio-political and socio-cultural context in which they live.

Social Psychological Adjustment to School

The classroom behaviour of early total immersion and extended-core programs in the Ottawa Roman Catholic Separate School Board

(EDWARDS & SMYTH, 1976a), has been assessed through teacher ratings up to the grade 5 level. (The extended-core program begins in grade 1 and usually involves teaching one subject area in French along with French language arts for an extended period of 60 to 75 minutes.) Three subtests of the Pupil Rating Scale (MYKLEBUST, 1971) were used: auditory comprehension, spoken language, and personal-social behaviour. The results, summarized in EDWARDS, COLLETTA, FU & McCARREY (1979a), show that the teachers either tend not to find any differences between the two groups or tend to favour the early immersion group. This suggests that the early immersion children did not have any noticeable difficulty adjusting to their school experience.

Another way of approaching the issue of adjustment to school is to question students directly about their current program, about the type of program they would have preferred, and about the type of program they would prefer in the future.

Using a questionnaire, LAMBERT & TUCKER (1972) asked grade 4 and 5 students who had been in the St. Lambert early total immersion program and their English-educated comparison groups who had studied core French from grade 1 on to express their opinions about the French programs they were enrolled in. For example, they asked them, "Do you enjoy studying French the way you do at your school?" Forty-five per cent of the grade 4 and 52% of the grade 5 immersion children responded, "I enjoy it very much", whereas only 18% of the grade 4 and 16% of the grade 5 core French children answered in this way. When asked, "Would you rather go to an all-English school?", 3% of the grade 4 and 4% of the grade 5 immersion students responded with "Yes, I would very much", whereas 31% of the grade 4 and 46% of the grade 5 children answered in this way. At the other end of the scale, 75% of the grade 4 and 68% of the grade 5 immersion students responded, "I enjoy school as it is". Only 31% of the grade 4 and 27% of the grade 5 core French students said that they enjoyed school as it was. The students were also asked, "In your opinion, is too much time spent on French?" Seventy-five per cent of the grade 4 and 80% of the grade 5 immersion children agreed that "Just about the right amount of time is spent on French", whereas 63% of the grade 4 and 37% of the grade 5 core French children agreed with this statement. Finally, when asked, "Do you want to continue learning French?", the immersion students were more likely to answer, "Yes, I want to very much" (70% in grade 4 and 84% in grade 5) than were the core French students (55% in grade 4 and 37% in grade 5). Indeed, 12% of the grade 4 and 19% of the grade 5 core French students responded, "I don't really want to learn French anymore", whereas virtually none of the immersion students answered in this way.

These figures suggest a general endorsement by immersion students of their program and their mode of French study.

The grade 5 students who filled out questionnaires in the study discussed above and who could be located in their graduating year (grade 11), were sent another questionnaire and were also interviewed in their homes with their parents (CZIKO *et al.*, 1978). In general it was found that "there is a very clear appreciation for the early immersion experience on the part of the early immersion students and their parents who, in the vast majority, say that they would choose the immersion option if they had to do it all over" (p. 23). Furthermore,

> "Having experienced immersion schooling, both the early immersion students and their parents are more inclined to see the merits of going even further in forms of immersion to the point of full contact with French students in French language schools. Rather than viewing 'submersion' in a total French school as a radical step, one that might adversely affect a child's identity and native language competence, it is seen more as a natural and obvious extension of early immersion by a substantial number of early immersion students and their parents." (CZIKO *et al.*, 1978:24).

Thus, the results of the St. Lambert study suggest that early immersion students and their parents are generally satisfied with the program and take as natural and appropriate the idea of going a step further towards integrated schooling in the other language community.

In Ontario, grade 8 students in the Peel late immersion and in the Ottawa and Carleton early total immersion programs were asked about their program preferences (LAPKIN *et al.*, 1982), as were the grade 8 early immersion students and extended-core students of the Ottawa Separate Board (EDWARDS, COLLETTA, FU & McCARREY, 1979a). Direct comparison of results between the studies is difficult, because different ways of analysing the data were used. Nevertheless, the results show that the early immersion students in both studies were more likely to respond that they would prefer a bilingual high school program and that the amount of time spent in French during the school day was "about right" or "a bit too short". In contrast, the late immersion and extended-core students were more likely to respond that they would prefer a program with less French in it and that the amount of time spent in French was "a bit too long". These results indicate a greater satisfaction with their program among early immersion students than among late immersion or extended-core students at the grade 8 level. These results also suggest indirectly that the early total immersion students have made at least as satisfactory an adjustment to their school experience as students in other types of programs.

Social Psychological Perceptions

Virtually all the research pertaining to the feelings or attitudes of immersion students towards themselves, their own ethnic group, and other ethnic groups has been carried out in the Montreal area. Were similar studies carried out in other cities in Canada, the results might differ somewhat. It is our opinion, however, that the results related to the immersion students' feelings about themselves and their own ethnic group would not differ in important ways. As for their attitudes towards the target language group (French-Canadians), the Montreal setting may well influence the results. Nevertheless, we consider the findings to be of considerable interest in demonstrating the impact of immersion schooling in a particular milieu.

There are several reasons why one might expect the learning of a second language to have an effect on the social psychological make-up of an individual. For example, learning a second language permits the possibility of contact with, and therefore possible socialization by, another cultural group (GENESEE, 1980b). The nature of the contact and the status of the language/culture, among other things, will influence the precise effects of the contact, and this is why we might expect to find differences between English speakers learning French in Montreal and, for example, in Toronto or Vancouver. Furthermore, to the extent that language is seen as an important symbol of ethnicity, then learning a second language might influence one's perception of oneself and/or one's perception of the target language group.

Perception of self and own ethnolinguistic group

In the early grades (2 to 5) of the St. Lambert study, the French immersion and English comparison groups were asked to rate themselves and English-Canadians on 13 bipolar dimensions such as friendly/unfriendly, industrious/lazy, and calm/emotional (LAMBERT & TUCKER, 1972). The immersion and comparison groups both made favourable assessments of themselves and of English-Canadians.

In another study probing the ethnic identities of immersion children, GENESEE, TUCKER & LAMBERT (1978a) used a doll preference technique in which the child is asked to indicate how similar (dissimilar) he/she is to each of a number of dolls that represent different ethnolinguistic groups. English-speaking students in English schools, French schools, and immersion schools from grades 1 to 5 were tested. The children in all three types of programs and at all grade levels indicated the same degree of English-Canadian identity.

Another technique used in studies of social perception, known as multidimensional scaling, asks respondents to rate pairs of concepts such as "myself" and "monolingual English-Canadians" in terms of their perceived similarity/dissimilarity. The grounds for making these judgments are left to the respondent. Analysis of the judgments using multidimensional scaling summarizes and graphically describes the perceived similarities/dissimilarities, as well as the dimensions used in making judgments. This technique then yields a type of psychological map of the student's social world.

CZIKO, LAMBERT & GUTTER (1979) used this technique by having groups of children make judgments of degrees of similarity among ten relevant concepts: monolingual English-Canadians, bilingual English-Canadians, monolingual French-Canadians, bilingual French-Canadians, Italian-Canadians, English people from England, French people from France, Americans, your teacher, and yourself. Eight groups of students were involved in the study: grade 5 and grade 6 students in an English program; grade 5 and grade 6 students in an early total immersion program; grade 5 and grade 6 students in a "late" immersion program; and grade 5 and grade 6 French students in a French school. The "late" immersion students had participated in a one-year French immersion program at grade 4.

Two major clusters of concepts were identifiable in the students' responses: one related to the English language and English-Canadians, and another related to the French language and French-Canadians. The immersion students (early and late) and the English program students both perceived themselves to fall within the English cluster. However, the early immersion students perceived themselves as more similar to bilingual English-Canadians and bilingual French-Canadians than did the late immersion or English program students. The authors conclude: ". . . the early immersion experience seems to have reduced the social distance between self and French-Canadians, especially French-Canadians who are bilingual" (CZIKO, LAMBERT & GUTTER, 1979:26). GENESEE (1977b) also found (using multidimensional scaling) that grade 6 early immersion students perceived less social distance between themselves and French-Canadians than did grade 6 English program students. In a related vein, LAMBERT & TUCKER (1972) asked grade 4 and 5 immersion and English-educated (with core French component) children in the St. Lambert study: "After studying French for several years . . . do you think you have become less English-Canadian in your thoughts and feelings; or do you see yourself now as being both English- *and* French-Canadian, or as more English-Canadian?", 65% of the grade 4 and 66% of the grade 5 immersion children responded, "both English and French", while 27% of the grade 4 and 13% of the grade 5 English-educated group responded in this way.

In summary, it appears that immersion students maintain a basic identity with an English ethnolinguistic reference group (GENESEE, 1977b). However, early immersion students tend to see themselves as more like French-Canadians than do late immersion or English program students, thus reducing the perceived English-Canadian/French-Canadian gulf to a significant degree.

Perception of target language group

In the St. Lambert studies in which LAMBERT & TUCKER (1972) had early total immersion and English comparison groups rate themselves and English-Canadians on 13 bipolar dimensions, they also had the students rate French-Canadians and European French people. It was found that the French immersion children in the early grades (2–3) had more favourable attitudes towards French-Canadians and European French people than did the English-educated comparison group. However, there were no such differences found between the same groups of children at later grades (4 and 5).

Nevertheless, when the same grade 5 immersion and English comparison students were asked *directly* about their feelings and attitudes towards French-speaking people, the immersion students were clearly more positive. For example, when asked, "Since you have been learning about French people at school, do you like French-Canadians more now than you did before?", 64% of the grade 5 immersion students responded, "I like them more now than I did before", whereas only 15% of the English comparison group responded in this way. Similarly, when asked, "Suppose you happened to be born into a French-Canadian family would you be just as happy to be a French-Canadian as an English-Canadian person?", 84% of the grade 5 immersion children responded, "just as happy to be French-Canadian", whereas only 48% of the English-educated group responded in this way.

When the same grade 5 immersion and comparison children were sent questionnaires and were interviewed in grade 11, their graduating year, it was found that the early total immersion students showed a more positive attitude towards French-Canadians, used French more frequently with their French friends, and were more willing to make use of French in their contacts with the French-speaking community than were the English comparison students (CZIKO, *et al.*, 1978; see also GENESEE, 1980a).

Other studies have examined the attitudes of both early and late immersion students towards French-Canadians, using techniques similar to those used by LAMBERT & TUCKER (1972); e.g. CZIKO, HOLOBOW & LAMBERT (1977a, b); CZIKO, HOLOBOW, LAMBERT & TUCKER (1977); GENESEE, MORIN & ALLISTER (1974a); GENESEE, POLICH & STANLEY (1976). In general, the results show that in the first year or two of the immersion program, the attitudes of the immersion students may be more positive towards French-Canadians than those of the English comparison groups. However, in later years of the program, the immersion students fail to express significantly more positive attitudes than non-immersion students. Nevertheless, in no case have the attitudes of immersion students towards French-Canadians been less favourable than those of their English-educated comparison group.

> "It may be that the attitudes of immersion students, although initially more positive, come to be the same as those of students in a regular program since there is an absence of real social contact with members of the target language, and a lack of behavioural or social evidence on which to sustain positive attitudes beyond introductory immersion." (GENESEE, 1980b:16)

The lack of sustained contact with members of the target language group that GENESEE refers to is a problem which, for different reasons than in Montreal, faces most immersion students in many Canadian cities. In these cities, the francophone population is small, and contact with francophones is difficult to establish in French because they are so fluently bilingual (SWAIN, 1981b). This lack of contact may affect not only the failure to generate more positive attitudes, but also the failure to make significant progress beyond a certain plateau in speaking French (see Chapter 4 for details).

Although the results from the studies noted above using highly evaluative attitudinal measures have tended to show no differences between the immersion and non-immersion groups after a year or so of the immersion program, we have seen that in other studies where similarity/dissimilarity judgments have been used (e.g. CZIKO, LAMBERT & GUTTER, 1979; GENESEE, 1977b), early French immersion students tend to view themselves as less different from French-Canadians than do non-immersion students.

"It may be that the immersion students' familiarization with French-Canadians through interaction with French-speaking teachers and through exposure to curricular material in French has made them realize fundamental similarities between the two ethnolinguistic groups that might otherwise be masked by more superficial language differences. The development of this kind of non-evaluative but socially-relevant perspective could be an important precursor for establishing positive intergroup attitude and/or social contact with members of the other group." (GENESEE, 1980b:18)

Socio-political and socio-cultural perceptions of Canada

It is possible that the educational experience of the immersion students might lead to a more sophisticated understanding of socio-political relations between the French and English, as well as of the socio-cultural mosaic of Canada in general.

To investigate the latter question, grade 5 and 6 early total immersion students and their English-educated peers in Ottawa and Toronto were asked to write a composition on the topic of "why I like (or do not like) being Canadian" (SWAIN, 1980a). Each composition was subjected to a content analysis and the substantive comments that had been written were identified and tabulated. Several interesting findings emerge from this study. First, the immersion students' commentary spanned a much broader perspective; that is, the immersion children in grade 5 gave twice as many reasons for why they liked being Canadian as did their English-educated peers, and the immersion children in grade 6 gave three times as many reasons as their English-educated peers. Second, among the reasons given, over 30% of the immersion children (as compared to approximately 10% of the regular program students) commented specifically on the rich and varied cultural and/or linguistic composition of Canada. For example, one grade 5 student wrote:

"I like being Canadian because we have people from all over the world who may live just next door. Here in Canada you hear different languages and styles . . . And most of all we care."

Similarly, over 20% of the immersion children, but none of the English-educated children, commented on the possibility in Canada of being able to speak more than one language, and how they appreciated the opportunity. In general, most of the compositions written by the English-educated students focussed on the natural beauty of Canada as opposed to the "beauty" of linguistic and cultural diversity which was more likely to be emphasized in the total immersion students' compositions.

Along a similar line, BLAKE *et al.* (undated) gave students a choice of topics to write about, including: "What are, in your opinion, the two most important problems between English-speaking and French-speaking Canadians?" and "If you feel that there are difficulties between English-speaking and French-speaking Canadians . . . what could be done so that English- and French-speaking Canadian young people would get along better?" The students involved in this study were bilingual and essentially unilingual anglophone and francophone students at the grade 6 and 11 levels. The bilingual anglophone students had participated in a French immersion program from Kindergarten or grade 1 on. The discussion of the results is limited below to those of the grade 11 students. The problem cited most frequently by the students was language differences, and it was the unilingual francophone group in particular who stressed this problem. They also cited differences in customs and culture as a problem at least twice as frequently as the other three grade 11 groups. The unilingual anglophone group, on the other hand, cites the issue of pressure towards separation and national disunity at least twice as frequently as the other groups. Thus, although the possibility of separation may underlie political differences, it may be significant that the immersion students are less likely than the unilingual English students to mention this possibility specifically.

The bilingual groups — francophone and anglophone — cited the segregation of the two groups, stubbornness and resistance to getting along as problems much more frequently than the unilingual groups.

The differences among the groups in the solutions they offered are interesting. The bilingual students suggested solutions involving greater intergroup contact much more frequently than the unilingual students. The immersion students suggested more frequently than all other groups that emphasis be placed on mixing anglophones and francophones in bilingual schools, and on learning about one another's culture. The bilingual francophones, on the other hand, more frequently suggested exchange programs in which students live for a short time in each other's homes as a means of achieving greater intergroup contact. The authors conclude:

> ". . . having mastered the fundamentals of the other group's
> language and way of life, the bilingual can then see beyond the
> simple solution of language competence as a determiner of
> intergroup harmony to the more basic need of integrating with,
> going to school with and interacting with the other group . . . the
> bilinguals may be more sophisticated in the solutions they

suggest for reducing intergroup tensions because of their knowledge of and sensitivity to the other group's point of view." (BLAKE, *et al.*, undated:24)

It is also a sign of their sophistication that the bilinguals were more likely to see one of the major problems as segregation rather than separation.

Conclusions

In this chapter we have looked at some social and psychological aspects of immersion education. First, the adjustment made by immersion children to their school experience was examined by looking at studies of the children's behaviour in class and their views about their school program. The results suggest that early immersion students adjust readily to their school environment, and report satisfaction with their program and their way of studying French — more so than do late immersion students, or students studying core French in short daily periods.

Second, the feelings that immersion students hold towards themselves, their own ethnic group, and the target language group were examined. The findings, mostly from early total immersion students in the Montreal area, indicate that early immersion students view themselves, English-Canadians, and French-Canadians in at least as positive a light as do their English-educated counterparts; and sometimes more positively, although this effect may be limited to the initial year or two of immersion schooling unless sustained contact with target group members occurs. Nevertheless, early total immersion students tend to see themselves as more similar to French-Canadians than do their English-speaking peers, suggesting that immersion students have developed less rigid ethnolinguistic stereotypes of target group members.

Third, the socio-political and socio-cultural views of early total immersion students were examined. Immersion students in Ontario are more likely to comment on Canada as a nation of rich linguistic and cultural heritage than their English-educated counterparts. Immersion students in Montreal, along with their bilingual francophone peers, are more likely to see the problems facing English- and French-Canadians in terms of segregation rather than separation, separation being how their unilingual peers characterize the problem. Furthermore, bilingual students tend to see greater interethnic contact as the key to the solution of French-English tensions in Canada.

Whether the immersion students' views are the result of their schooling experience, the influence of their parents, or their experience in the wider community cannot be determined from the studies undertaken. Probably their views reflect the interaction of all three. Practically speaking, the source of their views is probably less important than their existence, which can be looked upon as a potentially positive force in Canada today.

7   Summary and Conclusions

Much has been learned about immersion education in Ontario over the last ten years. In this book, three alternative approaches to French immersion education have been discussed. The three program variations make available to an increasing number of English-speaking students in Ontario and throughout Canada the opportunity to reach advanced levels of French proficiency while studying the same school curriculum content as they would in a regular English program.

The evaluation of early total, early partial, and late immersion programs by the Bilingual Education Project in the Modern Language Centre at OISE began in 1970 and testing continued until 1979. In discussing the findings, not only the answers provided by the research have been summarized, but also some of the questions which remain unanswered have been identified.

One of these questions was discussed in Chapter 2. Although a small number of studies confirm that the immersion approach, emphasizing the communication of meaningful content material through French, is being put into practice in early and late immersion classrooms, much work remains to be done in this area. For example, effective teaching strategies in immersion classrooms need to be identified and described. This information would be useful not only as input to teacher training programs, but would also serve to broaden our understanding of the processes of second language learning.

In Chapter 3, the research questions reflecting the concerns of parents and educators were reviewed. The tests, procedures, and design used in the research were discussed and some comments with respect to their relative strengths and weaknesses were made. The design of the research conducted by the Bilingual Education Project allows for questions to be answered of the sort: "How do French immersion students perform on tests in English relative to students educated in English with similar socio-economic and IQ characteristics?"; "How do immersion students perform on tests of French proficiency relative to core French students, to other immersion students, and/or to francophone students?" The design also allowed for an assessment of the same group of immersion students as it progressed through the grades, as well as an assessment of new groups of immersion students taking the program in succeeding years.

Chapter 4 provides an overview of the linguistic outcomes associated with the three French immersion alternatives evaluated by the Bilingual Education Project. Listed below are the conclusions that one can draw, based on a synthesis of all available information, including evaluations conducted by other researchers in Ontario and throughout Canada.

1. In the area of English language skills (related to literacy), immersion students in all three programs exhibit temporary lags relative to the performance of regular English program groups. In early total and early partial immersion, the immersion students' weaker performance lasts until about the end of grade 3, whereas for late immersion the lag is shorter, or does not occur at all. The overall trend in subsequent grades is for immersion students to perform as well as or, in the case of early total immersion students, better than their English-educated counterparts. No such lags are evident in the oral/aural use of English.

2. As far as French skills are concerned, early total immersion students attain near-native proficiency in listening and reading comprehension, and achieve as well as an average class of francophone students in Montreal on a French achievement test. Their productive skills, speaking and writing, remain non-native-like, although they have little difficulty in conveying what they want to say.

3. Early partial French immersion produces less dramatic results in that it takes longer for the students to match the performance of early total immersion groups. By grade 8, however, based on the very limited data from one class in Elgin County, the performance of early partial immersion students resembles that of grade 7 early total immersion students on tests given in common.

4. The French skills of late immersion students appear to remain well below those of francophone comparison groups, even after several years of immersion. When the performance of Ontario late immersion

students at grade 8 after one, two, or three years in the program is compared with that of early total immersion students at the same grade level, the early immersion groups are well ahead.

5. The perceptions and self-assessments of grade 8 immersion students' French correspond to the findings summarized in (4) above. Early total immersion students consider themselves more skilled in French than late immersion students do and would prefer to spend a greater percentage of their school day studying in French.

6. In the evaluations of the three immersion program alternatives, comparisons with the French performance of core French students have revealed that the immersion students' performance is almost always significantly better than that of core French students.

7. Final comparisons of the French proficiency of early and late immersion students in Ontario must be deferred until the early immersion groups have reached the end of secondary school. A preliminary consideration of relevant findings from Montreal suggests that the design of each program (e.g. intensity of exposure to French at particular levels) is a key factor.

8. The level of French skills attained by students in immersion programs may also be related to the school setting. Thus, findings from one study suggest that the program in an immersion centre where no regular English program exists produces better results (superior French listening and reading scores, for example) than housing it in a dual-track school.

9. Early total immersion students' spoken French is generally assessed favourably by francophone adults and children. Their patterns of French language use, however, indicate that they tend not to seek out opportunities for using their second language skills, but respond in French when conversation is initiated in French. This appears to hold for both early and late immersion students, who differ, however, in terms of their use of French in the classroom with the teacher. In the latter context, early immersion students report a significantly greater use of French.

10. The ability to learn to communicate functionally in the second language is not related to intelligence as measured by standardized IQ tests.

Achievement in school subjects such as mathematics, science, and social studies is the subject of Chapter 5, where results from relevant content testing are reviewed. It may be unfair to test students from partial immersion programs (both early and late) in French, as they may not have a sufficiently high level of proficiency in the second language to permit them to demonstrate their knowledge of or skills in particular subject areas. Early total immersion students, however, appear able to cope equally well with tests of subject matter achievement administered in French or in English. The conclusions that may be drawn with respect to the academic outcomes of immersion programs are listed below.

1. Immersion education has not had negative effects on the students' general intellectual development, and, in the case of early total French immersion, may lead to its enhancement.

2. In mathematics, science, and social studies early total immersion students generally achieve as well as students studying these subjects in English. Early partial and late immersion students appear occasionally to have some difficulty relative to their comparison groups in acquiring mathematical and science skills. The difficulty experienced may be related to limitations experienced because of weaker second language skills.

3. The work-study skills of early total immersion students tend to be superior to those of their English-educated peers. No such trends are noticeable in the results of early partial immersion students.

In Chapter 6, studies of social and psychological aspects of immersion education were presented, much of the data coming from Montreal. The results indicate that early immersion students adjust smoothly to their school environment, and are more satisfied with their program than are late immersion students. Most of the studies reviewed concerned early immersion students: in general their self-concept is positive; they feel themselves to be English-Canadians rather than French-Canadians, but tend to develop less rigid ethnolinguistic stereotypes than their English-educated counterparts. Immersion students favour increased contact with francophones, a step which is likely to prove beneficial not only for developing more positive attitudes, but also for enhancing French language skills.

There seems little question that all three immersion programs have proven successful in promoting advanced French language skills, and that immersion constitutes a viable alternative form of education in Ontario and elsewhere in Canada.

Implications

In Chapter 1 we listed four characteristics of Canadian French immersion education which have contributed to its success:

1. parental involvement in establishing and ensuring the continuation of the immersion programs,

2. the majority group membership of the participating students and parents,

3. positive attitudes towards French and French-Canadians, and

4. the optional nature of the program.

Where these four factors are present, any of the immersion alternatives described in this study can be implemented with a high likelihood of success. In the absence of one or more of these factors, the likelihood of successful outcomes may be reduced. For example, in the case of bilingual education for minority groups, initial education in the second lanauge may, due to a lack of support for the first language, lead to first language loss and eventually to unilingualism in the second language, rather than bilingualism in the home and school languages. The success of the immersion approach for majority children can be explained in part by the fact that their home language, English, has been strongly supported in their home and environment before they enter a program in which French is the medium of instruction. By analogy, then, in the absence of environmental support the home language of minority language children should continue to be developed at school before these students are required to function in a second language (see, for example, SWAIN, 1982). An early emphasis on the home language for minority language bilingual program students reinforces not only their linguistic development, but also the prestige of the first language both psychologically and sociologically.

For many minority language parents, education in the home language may appear counter-intuitive in the sense that they may believe that their children's acquisition of the second language will be slowed. Therefore it may be important to hold public meetings in several languages to reach potential bilingual program parents, and to provide information materials in the language(s) of the community. The attempt to communicate with relevant minority groups in their own language and in appropriate contexts (e.g. orally, in the case of non-literate parents) transmits the message that their language and culture are valued by the majority group.

The third ingredient for success is the existence of positive attitudes towards the target language and culture. In bilingual education for minority groups, while there is an economic incentive and social pressure to learn the majority language, there may also be an ambivalence on the part of the minority group towards the target language group (see CUMMINS, 1981c).

Finally, the optional nature of the program should, if possible, be maintained. In the Canadian experience, immersion programs have proved viable as attractive *alternatives* to the regular English program, in part because of the research comparing the outcomes of the two programs. By extension, the implementation of any new bilingual program should ideally be accompanied by research designed to evaluate its effects.

Bibliography

The Bibliography includes a comprehensive listing of reports, articles, and books which relate to immersion education in Canada and the United States. Those titles which are preceded by an asterisk have been referred to in the text.

ADAMS, D.R. 1976, L'école bilingue: Report of a three-year study of an elementary school immersion project. Research Report 76–13. Vancouver, B.C.: Evaluation and Research Education Services Group, Board of School Trustees, (mimeo).

ADIV, E. 1979a, Survey of students switching out of immersion and post-immersion programs. Montreal, Que.: Protestant School Board of Greater Montreal, (mimeo).

ADIV, E. 1979b, A comparison of early immersion and classes d'accueil programs at the kindergarten level. Montreal, Que.: Protestant School Board of Greater Montreal, (mimeo).

ADIV, E. 1980a, A comparison of second language performance in two alternative French immersion programs. Montreal, Que.: Protestant School Board of Greater Montreal, (mimeo).

ADIV, E. 1980b, An analysis of second language performance in two types of immersion programs. Ph.D. thesis, McGill University.

*ADIV, E. 1980c, A comparative evaluation of three French immersion programs: Grades 10 and 11. Paper presented at the Fourth Annual Convention of the Canadian Association of Immersion Teachers, (mimeo).

ADIV, E., & BUTEAU, M. 1980, A French-Hebrew immersion model in a multicultural environment. *Multiculturalism*, 4(2), 27–30.

*ADIV, E., & MORCOS, C. 1979, A comparison of three alternative French immersion programs at the grade 9 level. Montreal, Que.: Protestant School Board of Greater Montreal, (mimeo).

ADIV, E., & MORCOS, C. 1980, A comparison of three alternative French immersion programs. Montreal, Que.: Protestant School Board of Greater Montreal, (mimeo).

ANDREW, C.M., LAPKIN, S., & SWAIN, M. 1979a, Report on the 1978 evaluation of the Ottawa and Carleton French immersion programs, grades 5–7. Toronto, Ont.: Ontario Institute for Studies in Education, (mimeo).

ANDREW, C.M., LAPKIN, S., & SWAIN, M. 1979b, Report on the 1978 evaluation of the French immersion program at Allenby Public School in Toronto, grades 4–6. Toronto, Ont.: Ontario Institute for Studies in Education, (mimeo).

ANDREW, C.M., LAPKIN, S., & SWAIN, M. 1979c, Report to the Elgin County Board of Education on the 1978 evaluation of the partial French immersion programs in grades 3, 6, 7 and 8. Toronto, Ont.: Ontario Institute for Studies in Education, (mimeo).

ANDREW, C.M., LAPKIN, S., & SWAIN, M. 1980a, Report on the 1979 evaluation of a French immersion program and an extended French program in the Toronto Board of Education, grades 5–8. Toronto, Ont.: Ontario Institute for Studies in Education, (mimeo).

ANDREW, C.M., LAPKIN, S., & SWAIN, M. 1980b, Report to the Peel County Board of Education on the 1978 evaluation of the late French immersion (LFI) program in grades 8, 11, 12 and 13. Toronto, Ont.: Ontario Institute for Studies in Education, (mimeo).

*BARIK, H.C. 1975, *French Comprehension Test, Level 1* (Test and Teacher's Manual). Toronto, Ont.: Ontario Institute for Studies in Education, (Teacher's Manual revised, 1976.)

*BARIK, H.C. 1976, *French Comprehension Test, Primer* (Test and Test Manual). Toronto, Ont.: Ontario Institute for Studies in Education.

BARIK, H.C. & SWAIN, M. 1974, English-French bilingual education in the early grades: The Elgin study. *Modern Language Journal,* 58, 392–403.

BARIK, H.C., & SWAIN, M. 1975a, Three-year evaluation of a large scale early grade French immersion program: The Ottawa study. *Language Learning,* 25, 1–30.

BARIK, H.C., & SWAIN, M. 1975b, Early grade French immersion classes in a unilingual English Canadian setting: The Toronto study. *Scientia Paedagogica Experimentalis,* 12, 153–177.

BARIK, H.C., & SWAIN, M. 1976a, Programmes d'immersion en français en Ontario: résultats d'une étude. *Bulletin de la F.I.P.F.* (Fédération internationale des professeurs de français), 12–13, 75–83.

BARIK, H.C., & SWAIN, M. 1976b, Primary-grade French immersion in a unilingual English-Canadian setting: The Toronto study through grade 2. *Canadian Journal of Education,* 1, 39–58.

BARIK, H.C., & SWAIN, M. 1976c, Update on French immersion: The Toronto study through grade 3. *Canadian Journal of Education,* 1, 33–42.

BARIK, H.C., & SWAIN, M. 1976d, English-French bilingual education in the early grades: The Elgin study through grade four. *Modern Language Journal,* 60, 3–17.

BARIK, H.C., & SWAIN, M. 1976e, A Canadian experiment in bilingual education: The Peel study. *Foreign Language Annals,* 9, 465–479.

*BARIK, H.C., & SWAIN, M. 1976f, A longitudinal study of bilingual and cognitive development. *International Journal of Psychology,* 11, 251–263.

BARIK, H.C., & SWAIN, M. 1977a, French immersion in Canada: The Ottawa study through grade four. *ITL. A Review of Applied Linguistics,* 36, 45–70.

BARIK, H.C., & SWAIN, M. 1977b, Report to the Elgin County Board of Education re: Evaluation of the 1976–77 partial French immersion program in grades 5–7. Toronto, Ont.: Ontario Institute for Studies in Education, (mimeo).

BARIK, H.C., & SWAIN, M. 1978a, Evaluation of a French immersion program: The Ottawa study through grade five. *Canadian Journal of Behavioural Science*, 10, 192–201.

BARIK, H.C., & SWAIN, M. 1978b, Follow-up on French immersion: The Toronto study through grade four. *Scientia Paedogogica Experimentalis*, 15, 181–206.

BARIK, H.C., & SWAIN, M. 1978c, Report to the Toronto Board of Education re: Evaluation of the 1976–77 French immersion program in grades 3–5 at Allenby Public School. Toronto, Ont.: Ontario Institute for Studies in Education, (mimeo).

BARIK, H.C., & SWAIN, M. 1978d, Evaluation of a bilingual education program in Canada: The Elgin study through grade six. *Bulletin CILA*, 27, 31–58.

*BARIK, H.C., & SWAIN, M. (with SCHLOSS, B.) 1979, *Tests de Lecture: Tests of French Reading Comprehension for Grades 2–6*. Toronto, Ont.: Ontario Institute for Studies in Education.

BARIK, H.C., SWAIN, M., & GAUDINO, V. 1976, A Canadian experiment in bilingual education in the senior grades: The Peel study through grade 10. *International Review of Applied Psychology*, 25, 99–113.

BARIK, H.C., SWAIN, M., & McTAVISH, K. 1974, Immersion classes in an English setting: One way for les Anglais to learn French. *Working Papers on Bilingualism*, 2, 39–56.

BARIK, H.C., SWAIN, M., & NWANUNOBI, E. 1977, English-French bilingual education: The Elgin study through grade five. *Canadian Modern Language Review*, 33, 459–475.

BENSON, J.D., & GREAVES, W.S. 1981, You are not alone: Suzuki and French immersion. Paper presented at the 1981 International Suzuki Conference, University of Massachusetts at Amherst, July.

*BERKO, J. 1958, The child's learning of English morphology. *Word*, 14, 150–77.

BILASH, O. 1979/80, Bilingual education and Ukrainian Canadians. *Alberta Modern Language Journal*, 18(2), 24–30.

*BLAKE, L., LAMBERT, W.E., SIDOTI, N., & WOLFE, D. undated, Students' views of inter-group tensions in Quebec: The effects of language immersion experience. Montreal, Que.: McGill University, (mimeo).

BOYD, P.A. 1975, The development of grammar categories in Spanish by Anglo children learning a second language. *TESOL Quarterly*, 9, 125–135.

BRUCK, M. 1978, The suitability of early French immersion programs for the language disabled child. *Canadian Modern Language Review*, 34, 884–887.

BRUCK, M. 1979a, Switching out of French immersion. *Interchange*, 9, 86–94.

*BRUCK, M. 1979b, Problems in early French immersion programs. In B. MLACAK and E. ISABELLE (eds), *So You Want Your Child to Learn French!* Ottawa, Ont.: Canadian Parents for French, 42–47.

BRUCK, M. 1980, A longitudinal evaluation of the suitability of French immersion programs for the language disabled child: Progress from Kindergarten through grade 1. Montreal, Que.: McGill-Montreal Children's Hospital Learning Centre, (mimeo).

BRUCK, M., JAKIMIK, J., & TUCKER, G.R. 1975, Are French immersion programs suitable for working class children? A follow-up investigation. *Child Language*. Also in W. ENGLE, (ed.). Amsterdam, The Netherlands: Royal Vangorcum, 1976.

*Bruck, M., Lambert, W.E., & Tucker, G.R. 1974, Bilingual schooling through the elementary grades: The St. Lambert project at grade seven. *Language Learning*, 24, 183–204.

*Bruck, M., Lambert, W.E., & Tucker, G.R. 1975, Assessing functional bilingualism within a bilingual program: The St. Lambert project at grade eight. Montreal: Psychology Department, McGill University, (mimeo).

*Bruck, M., Lambert, W.E., & Tucker, G.R. 1976a, Cognitive and attitudinal consequences of bilingual schooling: The St. Lambert project through grade six. *International Journal of Psycholinguistics*, 6, 13–33.

Bruck, M., Lambert, W.E., & Tucker, G.R. 1976b, Alternative forms of immersion for second language teaching. *Working Papers on Bilingualism*, 10, 22–74.

Bruck, M., Rabinovitch, M.S., & Oates, M. 1975, The effects of French immersion programs on children with language disabilities: A preliminary report. *Working Papers on Bilingualism*, 5, 47–86.

Burns, G.E., & Olson, P. 1981, Implementation and Politics in French Immersion. Toronto, Ont.: Ontario Institute for Studies in Education.

Buteau, M., & Gougeon, H. 1973, Partial French immersion program, level 4: Pilot investigation. Beaconsfield, Que.: Lakeshore School Board Publications, (mimeo).

Buteau, M., & Gougeon, H. 1974, Evaluation of the 1973–1974 partial French immersion programs, second annual report. Beaconsfield, Que.: Lakeshore School Board Publications, (mimeo).

Buteau, M., & Gougeon, H. 1975, Evaluation of the 1974–1975 partial French immersion programs, third annual report. Beaconsfield, Que.: Lakeshore School Board Publications, (mimeo).

Buteau, M., & Gougeon, H. 1976, Evaluation of the 1975–1976 partial French immersion programs, fourth annual report. Beaconsfield, Que.: Lakeshore School Board Publications, (mimeo).

Buteau, M., & Gougeon, H. 1977, Evaluation of the 1976–1977 partial French immersion programs, fifth annual report. Beaconsfield, Que.: Lakeshore School Board Publications, (mimeo).

Buteau, M., & Gougeon, H. 1978, Evaluation of the 1977–1978 partial French immersion programs, sixth annual report. Beaconsfield, Que.: Lakeshore School Board Publications, (mimeo).

Buteau, M., & Gougeon, H. 1979, Partie française d'un programme experimental de maternelle bilingue. Montreal, Que.: Sainte-Croix School Board, (mimeo).

Buteau, M., & Gougeon, H. 1980a, A longitudinal evaluation of student achievement on English and French language tests. Paper presented at the Eastern Educational Research Association Annual Conference, Norfolk, Virginia, (mimeo).

Buteau, M., & Gougeon, H. 1980b, Evaluation of the St. Joseph of Mount Royal bilingual kindergarten program, first progress report. Montreal, Que.: Sainte-Croix School Board, (mimeo).

Buteau, M., & Gougeon, H. 1980c, Programme experimentale d'enseignement intégré des sciences humaines et du français en première année. Montreal, Que.: Sainte-Croix School Board, (mimeo).

BUTEAU, M., & GOUGEON, H. in press, Alternatives to traditional second-language education. In H.T. TRUEBA (ed.), *Bilingual Education: A Search for Theoretical Foundations*. Rowley, Mass.: Newbury House.

BUTRYM, L. 1978, Programme d'enseignement par immersion partielle IVe, Ve et VIe années. *Canadian Modern Language Review*, 34, 901–902.

CAMERON, A., FEIDER, H., & GRAY, V.A. 1974, Pilot evaluation of French Immersion grade 1 in Fredericton, N.B. Interim report, Spring, 1974. Fredericton, N.B.

CAMERON, C.A., & GRAY, V.A. 1976, Evaluation of an early French immersion education curriculum. Paper presented at International Congress of Psychology, Paris, (mimeo).

CAMERON, C.A., & GRAY, V.A. 1979, Summary report of 1978 French immersion evaluation. Fredericton, N.B., (mimeo).

CAMERON, C.A., GRAY, V.A., & FEIDER, H. 1975, Academic and linguistic achievement in a total French immersion elementary curriculum. Paper presented at Canadian Psychological Association, Quebec City, Quebec, June, (mimeo).

CAMPBELL, R.N., TAYLOR, D.M., & TUCKER, G.R. 1973, Teachers' views of immersion type bilingual programs: A Quebec example. *Foreign Language Annals*, 7, 106–110.

Canadian Modern Language Review (special issue), Bilingualism in education, 1974, 31, no. 2.

Canadian Modern Language Review (special issue), Proceedings of the first Canadian Association of Immersion Teachers/Association canadienne des professeurs d'immersion conference, 1978, 34, no. 5.

CAREY, S.T. (ed.) 1974, *Bilingualism, Biculturalism, and Education*. Edmonton, Alta.: University of Alberta Press.

CAREY, S.T. (guest ed.) 1978, Language acquisition and bilingualism in education. *Canadian Modern Language Review*, 34, entire no. 3.

CATHCART, R. 1972, Report on a group of Anglo children after one year of immersion in instruction in Spanish. M.A. thesis, University of California at Los Angeles.

*CHAUDRON, C. 1977a, Teacher's priorities in correcting learners' errors in French immersion classes. *Working Papers on Bilingualism*, 12, 21–44.

CHAUDRON, C. 1977b, A descriptive model of discourse in the corrective treatment of learners' errors. *Language Learning*, 22, 29–46.

CHUN, J. 1979, The importance of the language learning situation: Is immersion the same as the 'sink or swim method'? *Working Papers on Bilingualism*, 18, 131–164.

CITY OF HAMILTON BOARD OF EDUCATION, RESEARCH SERVICES DEPT. 1978, Evaluation of the French immersion program: An interim report after three years of the program. Hamilton, Ont.: Board of Education for the City of Hamilton, (mimeo).

CITY OF HAMILTON BOARD OF EDUCATION, RESEARCH SERVICES DEPT. 1979, An evaluation of the French immersion program: An annual report after four years of the program. Hamilton, Ont.: Board of Education for the City of Hamilton, (mimeo).

CLEGHORN, A. 1981, Patterns of teacher interaction in an immersion school in Montreal. Ph.D. thesis, McGill University.

COHEN, A.D. 1974a, The Culver City Spanish immersion program: The first two years. *Modern Language Journal*, 58, 95–103.

COHEN, A.D. 1974b, The Culver City Spanish immersion program: How does summer recess affect Spanish speaking ability? *Language Learning*, 24, 55–68.

COHEN, A.D. 1975a, Progress report on the Culver City Spanish immersion program: The third and fourth years. *Working Papers in Teaching English as a Second Language*, University of California at Los Angeles, 9, 47–65.

COHEN, A.D. 1975b, Forgetting a second language. *Language Learning*, 25, 127–138.

COHEN, A.D. 1975c, Successful immersion education in North America. *Working Papers on Bilingualism*, 5, 39–46.

COHEN, A.D. 1976a, The case for partial or total immersion education. In A. SIMOES (ed.), *Bilingual-Bicultural Education*. New York: Academic Press, 65–89.

COHEN, A.D. 1976b, The acquisition of Spanish grammar through immersion: Some findings after four years. *Canadian Modern Language Review*, 32, 562–574.

COHEN, A.D. 1979, Bilingual education for a bilingual community: Some insights gained from research. In R.V. PADILLA (ed.), *Bilingual Education and Public Policy in the U.S.* Ypsilanti, Mich.: Eastern Michigan University, 245–259.

COHEN, A.D. in press, Describing bilingual education classrooms: A guide for teachers, administrators, and evaluators. Rosslyn, Va.: National Clearinghouse for Bilingual Education.

COHEN, A.D., BRUCK, M., & RODRIGUEZ-BROWN, F.V. 1979, *Evaluating Evaluation. Bilingual Education Series No. 6*. Arlington, Va.: Center for Applied Linguistics.

COHEN, A.D., & LAOSA, L.M. 1979, Second language instruction: Some research considerations. In H.T. TRUEBA & C. BARNETT-MIZRAHI (eds), *Bilingual Multicultural Education and the Professional: From Theory to Practice*. Rowley, Mass.: Newbury House, 74–88.

COHEN, A.D., & SWAIN, M. 1976, Bilingual education: The immersion model in the North American context. *TESOL Quarterly*, 10, 45–54. Also in J.E. ALATIS & K. TWADDELL (eds), *English as a Second Language in Bilingual Education*. Washington, D.C.: TESOL, 1976, 55–63; and in J.B. PRIDE (ed.), *Sociolinguistic Aspects of Language Learning and Teaching*. London: Oxford University Press, 1979, 144–151.

CORLETT, C., FISH, S., McCALL, B., McKENZIE, C., OLIVER, E., & STEVENS, J. French immersion program: An evaluation of pupil skills. Guelph, Ont.: Wellington County Board of Education, (mimeo).

CORLETT, C., McKENZIE, C., & OLIVER, E. 1977, French immersion program: An evaluation of pupil skills and parent opinion. Guelph, Ont.: Wellington County Board of Education, (mimeo).

COWAN, J.R., & SARMED, Z. 1976, Reading performance of bilingual children according to type of school and home language. *Working Papers on Bilingualism*, 11, 75–114.

CRAWFORD, P. 1976, An evaluation of the French immersion program, kindergarten – grade two. Willowdale, Ont.: North York Board of Education, (mimeo).

CRAWFORD, P. 1979, Report on the 1979 evaluation of the French immersion program grades 2, 4, 5. Willowdale, Ont.: North York Board of Education, (mimeo).

CUMMINS, J. 1973, A theoretical perspective on the relationship between bilingualism and thought. *Working Papers on Bilingualism*, 1, 1-9.

CUMMINS, J. 1976, The influence of bilingualism on cognitive growth: A synthesis of research findings and explanatory hypotheses. *Working Papers on Bilingualism*, 9, 1-43.

CUMMINS, J. 1977a, Cognitive factors associated with the attainment of intermediate levels of bilingual skills. *Modern Language Journal*, 61, 3-12.

CUMMINS, J. 1977b, Immersion education in Ireland: A critical review of Macnamara's findings. *Working Papers on Bilingualism*, 13, 121-129.

CUMMINS, J. 1977c, A comparison of reading skills in Irish and English medium schools. In V. GREANEY (ed.), *Studies in Reading*. Dublin: Educational Co. of Ireland, 128-134.

CUMMINS, J. 1977d, Delaying native language reading instruction in immersion programs: A cautionary note. *Canadian Modern Language Review*, 34, 46-49.

CUMMINS, J. 1978a, Metalinguistic development of children in bilingual education programs: Data from Irish and Canadian (Ukrainian-English) programs. In M. PARADIS (ed.), *Aspects of Bilingualism*. Columbia, S.C.: Hornbeam Press, 127-138.

CUMMINS, J. 1978b, Bilingualism and the development of metalinguistic awareness. *Journal of Cross-Cultural Psychology*, 9, 131-149.

CUMMINS, J. 1978c, The cognitive development of children in immersion programs. *Canadian Modern Language Review*, 34, 855-883.

CUMMINS, J. 1978d, The cognitive development of bilingual children: A review of recent research. *Indian Journal of Applied Linguistics*, 4(2), 75-99.

CUMMINS, J. 1978e, Immersion programmes: The Irish experience. *International Review of Education*, 24, 273-282.

CUMMINS, J. 1978/79, Bilingualism and educational development in anglophone and minority francophone groups in Canada. *Interchange*, 9, 40-51.

CUMMINS, J. 1979a, Linguistic interdependence and the educational development of bilingual children. *Review of Educational Research*, 49, 222-251.

CUMMINS, J. 1979b, Should the child who is experiencing difficulties in early immersion be switched to the regular English program? A reinterpretation of Trites' data. *Canadian Modern Language Review*, 36, 139-143.

CUMMINS, J. 1979c, Cognitive/academic language proficiency, linguistic interdependence, the optimum age question and some other matters. *Working Papers on Bilingualism*, 19, 197-205.

*CUMMINS, J. 1979d, Cognitive development and early French immersion. In B. MLACAK & E. ISABELLE (eds), *So You Want Your Child to Learn French!* Ottawa, Ont.: Canadian Parents for French, 28-34.

CUMMINS, J. 1980a, Language proficiency, biliteracy and French immersion. Toronto, Ont.: Ontario Institute for Studies in Education, (mimeo).

CUMMINS, J. 1980b, The entry and exit fallacy in bilingual education. *NABE Journal*, 4, 25-59.

CUMMINS, J. 1981a, Effects of Kindergarten Experience on Academic Progress in French Immersion Programs. *Review and Evaluation Bulletins*, 2(6), Toronto: Ministry of Education, Ontario.

CUMMINS, J. 1981b, *Research findings from French immersion programs across Canada: A parents' guide*. In B.C. Ministry of Education, *Early French Immersion: Teacher's Resource Book*, Victoria: Ministry of Education, British Columbia, 21-30.

*CUMMINS, J. 1981c, The role of primary language development in promoting educational success for language minority students. In Office of Bilingual Bicultural Education (ed.), *Schooling and Language Minority Students: A Theoretical Framework*. Los Angeles, Calif.: Evaluation, Dissemination and Assessment Center, California State University, 3–49.

CUMMINS, J., & GULUTSAN, M. 1974, Bilingual education and cognition. *Alberta Journal of Educational Research*, 20, 259–269.

CUMMINS, J., & MULCAHY, R. 1978, Orientation to language in Ukrainian-English bilinguals. *Child Development*, 49, 479–482.

CZIKO, G.A. 1975, The effects of different French immersion programs on the language and academic skills of children from various socioeconomic backgrounds, M.A. thesis, McGill University.

CZIKO, G.A. 1976, The effects of language sequencing on the development of bilingual reading skills. *Canadian Modern Language Review*, 32, 534–539.

*CZIKO, G.A. 1978, Differences in first- and second-language reading: The use of syntactic, semantic and discourse constraints. *Canadian Modern Language Review*, 34, 473–489.

CZIKO, G.A. 1980, Language competence and reading strategies: A comparison of first- and second-language oral reading errors. *Language Learning*, 30, 101–116.

*CZIKO, G.A., HOLOBOW, N.E., & LAMBERT, W.E. 1977a, Early and late French immersion: A comparison of children at grade 7. Montreal, Que.: McGill University, (mimeo).

*CZIKO, G.A., HOLOBOW, N.E., & LAMBERT, W.E. 1977b, A comparison of three elementary school alternatives for learning French: Children at grades 4 and 5. Montreal, Que.: McGill University, (mimeo).

*CZIKO, G.A., HOLOBOW, N.E., LAMBERT, W.E., & TUCKER, G.R. 1977, A comparison of three elementary school alternatives for learning French: Children at grades 5 and 6. Montreal, Que.: McGill University, (mimeo).

*CZIKO, G.A., LAMBERT, W.E., & GUTTER, R. 1979, French immersion programs and students' social attitudes: A multidimensional investigation. *Working Papers on Bilingualism*, 19, 13–28.

*CZIKO, G.A., LAMBERT, W.E., SIDOTI, N., & TUCKER, G.R. 1978, Graduates of early immersion: Retrospective views of grade 11 students and their parents. Montreal, Que.: McGill University, (mimeo).

CZIKO, G.A., LAMBERT, W.E., SIDOTI, N., & TUCKER, G.R. 1979, Graduates of early immersion: Retrospective views of grade 11 students and their parents. In B. MLACAK & E. ISABELLE (eds), *So You Want Your Child to Learn French!* Ottawa, Ont.: Canadian Parents for French, 48–53.

D'ANGLEJAN, A., & TUCKER, G.R. 1971, Academic report: The St. Lambert program of home-school language switch. *Modern Language Journal*, 55, 99–101.

DAVINE, M., TUCKER, G.R., & LAMBERT, W.E. 1971, The perception of phoneme sequences by monolingual and bilingual school children. *Canadian Journal of Behavioural Science*, 3, 72–76.

DAY, E. 1978, Early immersion programs: A literature review. Burnaby, B.C.: Faculty of Education, Simon Fraser University, (mimeo).

DOCKRELL, W.B., & BROSSEAU, J.F. 1967, The correlates of second language learning by young children. *Alberta Journal of Educational Research*, 13, 295–298.

DONOGHUE, E., BENETEAU, Y., & MCINNIS, C.E. 1975, Experimental French programs in Carleton Roman Catholic Separate School Board. *Canadian Modern Language Review*, 31, 246–250.

DUHAMEL, R.J. 1976, Bilingual immersion. *Education Canada*, 16(1), 28–34.

DUMAS, G., SWAIN, M., & SELINKER, L. 1974, L'apprentissage du français langue seconde en classe d'immersion dans un milieu torontois. In S. CAREY (ed.), *Bilingualism, Biculturalism and Education*. Edmonton, Alta.: University of Alberta Press, 83–90.

DUMESNIL, L., & ROY, R.R. 1975, Elementary school French immersion program. *Manitoba Journal of Education*, 10, 29–31.

EDMONTON PUBLIC SCHOOLS. 1979, Implementation of bilingual (English-French) programs second year 1978–79. Edmonton, Alta.: Department of Research and Evaluation, Edmonton Public Schools, (mimeo).

*EDMONTON PUBLIC SCHOOLS. 1980, Implementation of bilingual (English-French) programs third year 1979–80. Edmonton, Alta.: Curriculum Department, Edmonton Public Schools, (mimeo).

EDWARDS, H.P. 1976, Evaluation of the French immersion program offered by the Ottawa Roman Catholic Separate School Board. *Canadian Modern Language Review*, 33, 137–150.

EDWARDS, H.P. 1979, An overview of French second-language programs. In B. MLACAK and E. ISABELLE (eds), *So You Want Your Child to Learn French!* Ottawa, Ont.: Canadian Parents for French, 9–11.

EDWARDS, H.P. 1980, Psychological and social psychological factors influencing second language acquisition. *Canadian Modern Language Review*, 36, 481–484.

EDWARDS, H.P., & CASSERLY, M.C. 1971, Research and evaluation of the French program. 1970–71 report: English schools. Ottawa, Ont.: Ottawa Roman Catholic Separate School Board, (mimeo).

EDWARDS, H.P., & CASSERLY, M.C. 1976, *Research and Evaluation of Second Language (French) Programs in the Schools of the Ottawa Roman Catholic Separate School Board (Annual reports 1971–72 and 1972–73)*. Toronto: Ministry of Education, Ontario.

*EDWARDS, H.P., COLLETTA, S., FU, L., & MCCARREY, H.A. 1979a, *Evaluation of the Federally and Provincially Funded Extensions of the Second Language Programs in the Schools of the Ottawa Roman Catholic Separate School Board: Annual Report 1978–79*. Toronto: Ministry of Education, Ontario.

EDWARDS, H.P., COLLETTA, S.P., FU, L., & MCCARREY, H.A. 1979b, Evaluation of second language program extensions offered in grades, 2, 3, 4, 9 and 10: Final report 1978–79. Ottawa, Ont.: Ottawa Roman Catholic Separate School Board, (mimeo).

EDWARDS, H.P., COLLETTA, S., FU, L., MCCARREY, H.A., & MCLAUGHLIN, M. 1978, Evaluation of the federally and provincially funded extensions of the second language programs in the schools of the Ottawa Roman Catholic Separate Board: Annual report 1977–78. Ottawa Roman Catholic Separate School Board, (mimeo).

*EDWARDS, H.P., DOUTRIAUX, C., FU, L., & MCCARREY, H.A. 1977, Evaluation of the federally and provincially funded extensions of the second language programs in the schools of the Ottawa Roman Catholic Separate School Board. Ottawa, Ont.: Ottawa Roman Catholic Separate School Board, (mimeo).

EDWARDS, H.P., DOUTRIAUX, C.W., & McCARREY, H.A. 1976, Evaluation of the grade one 50-50 bilingual program. Ottawa, Ont.: Ottawa Roman Catholic Separate School Board, (mimeo).

*EDWARDS, H.P., DOUTRIAUX, C.W., McCARREY, H.A., & FU, L. 1976, Evaluation of second language programs, English schools of the Ottawa Roman Catholic Separate School Board: Annual report 1975-76. Ottawa, Ont.: Ottawa Roman Catholic Separate School Board, (mimeo).

*EDWARDS, H.P., DOUTRIAUX, C.W., McCARREY, H.A., & FU, L. 1977, Evaluation of second language program extensions offered in grades 1, 2, 7 and 8: Final report 1976-77. Ottawa, Ont.: Ottawa Roman Catholic Separate School Board, (mimeo).

EDWARDS, H.P., FU, L., McCARREY, H.A., & DOUTRIAUX, C. 1981, Partial French immersion in grades one to four: The O.R.C.S.S.B. study. *Canadian Modern Language Review*, 37, 281-296.

*EDWARDS, H.P., McCARREY, H.A., & FU, L. 1980, Evaluation of second language program extensions offered in grades 3, 4, and 5 (English Schools, The Ottawa Roman Catholic Separate School Board): Final Report 1979-80. Ottawa, Ont.: Ottawa Roman Catholic Separate School Board, (mimeo).

*EDWARDS, H.P., McLAUGHLIN, M., McCARREY, H.A., & FU, L. 1978, Evaluation of second language program extensions offered in grades 2, 3, 8 and 9: Final report 1977-78. Ottawa, Ont.: The Ottawa Roman Catholic Separate School Board, (mimeo).

*EDWARDS, H.P., & SMYTH, F. 1976a, *Evaluation of Second Language Programs (Evaluation of Federally-Funded Extensions of Second Language Learning [French] Programs for the Ottawa Roman Catholic Separate School Board: Annual Reports 1973-74, 1974-75); and Some Alternatives for Teaching French as a Second Language in Grades Five to Eight.* Toronto, Ont.: Ministry of Education, Ontario.

EDWARDS, H.P., & SMYTH, F. 1976b, Alternatives to early immersion programs for acquisition of French as a second language. *Canadian Modern Language Review*, 32, 524-533.

ELLIS, A., FISH, S., McCALL, B., McKENZIE, C., OLIVER, E., & SMITH, G. 1979, French immersion program: An evaluation of pupil skills. Guelph, Ont.: Wellington County Board of Education, (mimeo).

EWANYSHYN, E. 1976, Evaluation of a Ukrainian-English bilingual program 1975-76. Edmonton, Alta.: Edmonton Catholic School System, (mimeo).

EWANYSHYN, E. 1978, Evaluation of a Ukrainian-English bilingual program 1976-77. Edmonton, Alta.: Edmonton Catholic School System, (mimeo).

EWANYSHYN, E. 1979, Evaluation of a Ukrainian-English bilingual program 1977-78. Edmonton, Alta.: Edmonton Catholic School System, (mimeo).

EWANYSHYN, E. 1980, Evaluation of a Ukrainian-English bilingual program 1978-79. Edmonton, Alta.: Edmonton Catholic School System, (mimeo).

FLORES, M. 1973, An early stage in the acquisition of Spanish morphology by a group of English-speaking children. M.A. thesis, University of California at Los Angeles.

FOIDART, D. 1981, Research and Evaluation of French Immersion Programmes in Man.: Preliminary Report. Winnipeg, Man.: Centre for Research and Consultation, (mimeo).

FRASURE SMITH, N., LAMBERT, W.E., & TAYLOR, D.M. 1975, Choosing the language of instruction for one's children: A Quebec study. *Journal of Cross-Cultural Psychology*, 6, 131–155.

GAME, A. 1979, The bilingual program (50/50): An alternative in the pursuit of bilingualism: Curriculum considerations. In B. MLACAK and E. ISABELLE (eds), *So You Want Your Child to Learn French!* Ottawa, Ont.: Canadian Parents for French, 66–73.

GENESEE, F. 1974a, Bilingual education – social psychological consequences. Ph.D. thesis, McGill University.

GENESEE, F. 1974b, Students' attitudes toward French immersion programs. Montreal, Que.: Protestant School Board of Greater Montreal, (mimeo).

*GENESEE, F. 1974c, An evaluation of the English writing skills of students in French immersion programs. Montreal, Que.: Protestant School Board of Greater Montreal, (mimeo).

GENESEE, F. 1976a, Comparative evaluation of the early French immersion, grade 7 French immersion and FSL programs: A follow-up study. Montreal, Que.: Protestant School Board of Greater Montreal, (mimeo).

GENESEE, F. 1976b, The suitability of French immersion programs for all children. *Canadian Modern Language Review*, 32, 494–515.

*GENESEE, F. 1976c, The role of intelligence in second language learning. *Language Learning*, 26, 267–280.

*GENESEE, F. 1976d, Addendum to the evaluation of the 1975-76 grade 11 French immersion class. Montreal, Que.: Protestant School Board of Greater Montreal, (mimeo).

GENESEE, F. 1977a, Schools, bilingualism and multiculturalism. Paper presented at the National Conference on Bilingualism and its Relationships to Multiculturalism, Winnipeg, Man., April.

*GENESEE, F. 1977b, French immersion and students' perceptions of themselves and others: An ethnolinguistic perspective. Montreal, Que.: Protestant School Board of Greater Montreal, (mimeo).

GENESEE, F. 1978a, Survey of students switching out of the early immersion program 1977-1978. Montreal, Que.: Instructional Services Dept., The Protestant School Board of Greater Montreal, (mimeo).

GENESEE, F. 1978b, Individual differences in second language learning. *Canadian Modern Language Review*, 34, 490–504.

GENESEE, F. 1978c, Is there an optimal age for starting second language instruction? *McGill Journal of Education*, 13, 145–154.

*GENESEE, F. 1978d, A longitudinal evaluation of an early immersion school program. *Canadian Journal of Education*, 3(4), 31–50.

GENESEE, F. 1978e, A survey of Canadian research on second language learning. *Second Language Acquisition Notes and Topics: A Newsletter for Researchers and Teachers*, 8, 1–31.

*GENESEE, F. 1978f, Second language learning and language attitudes. *Working Papers on Bilingualism*, 16, 19–42.

GENESEE, F. 1978/79, Scholastic effects of French immersion: An overview after ten years. *Interchange*, 9, 20–29.

GENESEE, F. 1979a, *Les programmes d'immersion en français du Bureau des Ecoles Protestantes du Grand Montreal*. Etudes et documents du Ministère de l'éducation du Québec; 1035, de la Chevrotière, Québec, Québec.

GENESEE, F. 1979b, Acquisition of reading skills in immersion programs. *Foreign Language Annals*, 12, 71–77.

GENESEE, F. 1979c, Beyond bilingualism: Some social aspects of French immersion. In B. MLACAK and E. ISABELLE (eds), *So You Want Your Child to Learn French!* Ottawa, Ont.: Canadian Parents for French, 35–41.

*GENESEE, F. 1979d, A comparison of early and late immersion programs. Montreal, Que.: McGill University, (mimeo).

*GENESEE, F. 1980a, Bilingualism and biliteracy: A study of cross-cultural contact in a bilingual community. In J. EDWARDS (ed.), *The Social Psychology of Reading*. Silver Spring, Md.: Institute of Modern Language, forthcoming.

*GENESEE, F. 1980b, Social psychological consequences of bilingualism. Paper presented at the Symposium on Standard Language/Vernacular Relations and Bilingual Education. Racine, Wisconsin, (mimeo).

GENESEE, F. 1981, Response to M. Swain: Linguistic environment as a factor in the acquisition of target language skills. In R. ANDERSON (ed.), *New Dimensions in Second Language Acquisition Research*.

GENESEE, F, ALLISTER, T., & MORIN, S. 1974a, Evaluation of the 1973–74 grade 7 French immersion class: February 1974. Montreal, Que.: Protestant School Board of Greater Montreal, (mimeo).

GENESEE, F., ALLISTER, T., & MORIN, S. 1974b, Evaluation of the 1973–74 pilot grade II French immersion class. Montreal, Que.: Protestant School Board of Greater Montreal, (mimeo).

GENESEE, F., & BOURHIS, R. 1979, Changing language norms and language use in Montreal. Montreal, Que.: McGill University, (mimeo).

GENESEE, F., & CHAPLIN, S. 1975a, A comparative evaluation of the Westmount Park French program, the early French immersion program and the FSL program at the grade 4 level. Montreal, Que.: Protestant School Board of Greater Montreal, (mimeo).

GENESEE, F., & CHAPLIN, S. 1975b, A comparison of the early French immersion, grade 7 French immersion and FSL programs at the grade 7 level: A preliminary report. Montreal, Que.: Protestant School Board of Greater Montreal, (mimeo).

GENESEE, F., & CHAPLIN, S. 1976a, Evaluation of the 1974–75 grade 5 French immersion class. Montreal, Que.: Protestant School Board of Greater Montreal, (mimeo).

GENESEE, F., & CHAPLIN, S. 1976b, Evaluation of the 1974–75 grade II French immersion class. Montreal, Que.: Protestant School Board of Greater Montreal, (mimeo).

GENESEE, F., & HAMAYAN, E. 1980, Individual differences in young second language learners. *Applied Psycholinguistics*, 1, 95–110.

GENESEE, F., & HOLOBOW, N. 1978, Children's reactions to variation in second language competence. In M. PARADIS (ed.), *Aspects of Bilingualism*. Hornbeam Press, 185–201.

GENESEE, F., & LAMBERT, W.E. 1980, Trilingual education for the majority group child. Montreal, Que.: McGill University, (mimeo).

GENESEE, F., LAMBERT, W.E., & TUCKER, G.R. 1978, An experiment in trilingual education: Report 4. *Language Learning*, 28, 343–365.

GENESEE, F., & LEBLANC, M. 1978, A comparative evaluation of three alternative French immersion programs: Grades 7 and 8. Montreal, Que.: Protestant School Board of Greater Montreal, (mimeo).

GENESEE, F., & MARCOS, C. 1978, A comparative evaluation of three alternative French immersion programs: Grades 8 and 9. Montreal, Que.: McGill University, (mimeo).

GENESEE, F., MORIN, S., & ALLISTER, T. 1974a, Evaluation of the 1973–74 pilot grade 7 French immersion class: June 1974. Montreal, Que.: Protestant School Board of Greater Montreal, (mimeo).

GENESEE, F., MORIN, S., & ALLISTER, T. 1974b, Evaluation of the 1973–74 grade 4 French immersion class. Montreal, Que.: Protestant School Board of Greater Montreal, (mimeo).

*GENESEE, F., POLICH, E., & STANLEY, M.H. 1977, An experimental French immersion program at the secondary school level: 1969–1974. *Canadian Modern Language Review*, 33, 318–332.

GENESEE, F., SHEINER, E., TUCKER, G.R., & LAMBERT, W.E. 1976, An experiment in trilingual education. *Canadian Modern Language Review*, 32, 115–128.

*GENESEE, F., & STANLEY, M.H. 1976, The development of English writing skills in French immersion programs. *Canadian Journal of Education*, 1(3), 1–17.

GENESEE, F., & STEFANOVIC, B. 1976a, Evaluation of the 1975–76 grade 6 French immersion class. Montreal, Que.: Protestant School Board of Greater Montreal, (mimeo).

GENESEE, F., & STEFANOVIC, B. 1976b, Evaluation of the 1975–76 grade II French immersion class: Cohort 3. Montreal, Que.: Protestant School Board of Greater Montreal, (mimeo).

GENESEE, F., & STEFANOVIC, B. 1976c, A sociolinguistic study of French language usage among French immersion students. Montreal, Que.: Protestant School Board of Greater Montreal, (mimeo).

GENESEE, F., & STEFANOVIC, B. 1976d, Evaluation of the Westmount Park enriched French program: A follow-up study. Montreal, Que.: Protestant School Board of Greater Montreal, (mimeo).

*GENESEE, F., TUCKER, G.R., & LAMBERT, W.E. 1975, Communication skills of bilingual children. *Child Development*, 46, 1010–1014.

GENESEE, F., TUCKER, G.R., & LAMBERT, W.E. 1976, Evaluation of the French, Hebrew and English language programs at Hebrew Foundation School and Solomon Schechter Academy: Report no. 2. Montreal, Que.: McGill University, (mimeo).

GENESEE, F., TUCKER, G.R., & LAMBERT, W.E. 1977, Communicational effectiveness of English children in French schools. *Canadian Journal of Education*, 2, 15–24.

*GENESEE, F., TUCKER, G.R., & LAMBERT, W.E. 1978a, The development of ethnic identity and ethnic role-taking skills in children from different school settings. *International Journal of Psychology*, 13, 39–57.

GENESEE, F., TUCKER, G.R., & LAMBERT, W.E. 1978b, An experiment in trilingual education: Report 3. *Canadian Modern Language Review*, 34, 621–643.

GRAY, V.A. 1978, Evaluation of early French immersion in Fredericton, N.B.: Grades three and four. Fredericton, N.B.: Psychology Dept., Univ. of New Brunswick, (mimeo).

GRAY, V.A. 1979, Evaluation of the French immersion programme in Fredericton, N.B.: Grades four and five. Fredericton, N.B.: Psychology Dept., Univ. of New Brunswick, (mimeo).

*GRAY, V.A. 1980, Evaluation of the French immersion programme in Fredericton, N.B.: Grades five and six. Fredericton, N.B.: Psychology Dept., Univ. of New Brunswick, (mimeo).

GRAY, V.A., & CAMERON, C.A. 1975, Evaluation of early French immersion in Fredericton, N.B.: Grades one and two. Fredericton, N.B.: Psychology Dept., Univ. of New Brunswick, (mimeo).

GRAY, V.A., & CAMERON, C.A. 1976, Evaluation of early French immersion in Fredericton, N.B.: Grades two and three. Fredericton, N.B.: Psychology Dept., Univ. of New Brunswick, (mimeo).

GRAY, V.A., & CAMERON, C.A. 1978, Summary report of French immersion evaluation, 1974–77. Fredericton, N.B.: Psychology Dept., Univ. of New Brunswick, (mimeo).

GRAY, V.A., & CAMERON, C.A. 1979, Grade one French immersion: A follow-up evaluation. Fredericton, N.B.: Psychology Dept., Univ. of New Brunswick, (mimeo).

GRAY, V.A., & CAMERON, C.A. 1980a, A follow-up evaluation of the fifth year of early French immersion. Fredericton, N.B.: Psychology Dept., Univ. of New Brunswick, (mimeo).

GRAY, V.A., & CAMERON, C.A. 1980b, A summary of the evaluation of the elementary French immersion programme, 1974–1979. Fredericton, N.B.: Psychology Dept., Univ. of New Brunswick, (mimeo).

GRAY, V.A., & CAMERON, C.A. 1980c, Longitudinal development of English morphology in French immersion children. *Applied Psycholinguistics*, 1, 171–181.

GRAY, V.A., CAMERON, C.A., & LINTON, M.J. 1976, A short-form test battery for evaluation of first year French immersion students. Fredericton, N.B.: Psychology Dept., Univ. of New Brunswick, (mimeo).

GROBE, C. undated, Mastery level for grade five French immersion students on the 1977 New Brunswick language arts criterion-referenced tests. N.B.: New Brunswick Dept. of Education, (mimeo).

GUNDEL, J.K., & TARONE, E. 1981, "Language transfer" and the acquisition of pronominal anaphora. Paper presented at the Ninth Conference on Applied Linguistics, Ann Arbor, Michigan, (mimeo).

HALPERN, G. 1976, Evaluation of French learning alternatives. *The Canadian Modern Language Review*, 33, 162–179.

HALPERN, G., HENDELMAN, T., KIRBY, D., MACNAB, G., MARTIN, C., TOURIGNY, R., & TUONG, T. 1974, The French Project: French Research and evaluation of numerous cogent hypotheses. Annual Report: Year One. (Carleton Board of Education/Ottawa Board of Education Report.)

HALPERN, G., MACNAB, G., & KIRBY, D. 1975, *Alternative school programs for French language learning. Evaluation of the Federally-Funded Extensions of the Second Language Learning (French) Programs in the Schools of the Carleton and Ottawa Boards of Education.* Toronto: Ministry of Education, Ontario.

HALPERN, G., MACNAB, G.L., KIRBY, D.M., TUONG, T.T., MARTIN, J.C., HENDELMAN, T., & TOURIGNY, R. 1976, *Alternative School Programs for French Language Learning: Evaluation of the Federally-Funded Extensions of the Second Language Learning (French) Programs in the Schools of the Carleton and the Ottawa Boards of Education.* Toronto: Ministry of Education, Ontario.

HALPERN, G., MARTIN, C., & KIRBY, D.M. 1976, Attrition rates in alternative primary school programs. *Canadian Modern Language Review*, 32, 516–523.

HAMAYAN, E. 1978, Acquisition of French syntactic structures: Production strategies and awareness of errors by native and non-native speakers. Ph.D. thesis, McGill University, Psychology Department.

HAMAYAN, E., GENESEE, F., & TUCKER, G.R. 1977, Affective factors and language exposure in second language learning. *Language Learning*, 27, 225–241.

HAMAYAN, E., MARKMAN, B., PELLETIER, S., & TUCKER, G.R. 1976, Differences in performance in elicited imitation between French monolingual and English speaking bilingual children. *Working Papers on Bilingualism*, 8, 30–58. Also published in *International Review of Applied Linguistics*, 1978, 16, 330–339.

HAMAYAN, E., & TUCKER, G.R. 1979, Strategies of communication used by native and non-native speakers of French. *Working Papers on Bilingualism*, 17, 83–96.

HAMAYAN, E., & TUCKER, G.R. 1980, Language input in the bilingual classroom and its relationship to second language achievement. Montreal: McGill University, (mimeo).

HARLEY, B. (guest ed.) 1976, Alternative programs for teaching French as a second language in the schools of the Carleton and Ottawa School Boards. *Canadian Modern Language Review*, 33, entire no. 2.

HARLEY, B. 1979, French gender 'rules' in the speech of English-dominant, French-dominant and monolingual French-speaking children. *Working Papers on Bilingualism*, 19, 129–156.

*HARLEY, B., & SWAIN, M. 1977, An analysis of verb form and function in the speech of French immersion pupils. *Working Papers on Bilingualism*, 14, 31–46.

*HARLEY, B., & SWAIN, M. 1978a, An analysis of the verb system used by young learners of French. *Interlanguage Studies Bulletin*, 3, 35–79.

HARLEY, B., & SWAIN, M. 1978b, Form and function in a second language: A close look at the verb system. Paper presented at the Fifth International Congress of Applied Linguistics, Montreal, (mimeo).

*HATCH, E. 1979, Simplified input and second language acquisition. Paper presented to the annual meeting of LSA, Los Angeles, (mimeo).

*HENDELMAN, T. 1975, History and geography test results of first year intermediate immersion classes and their comparisons, 1974–75. FRENCH Working Paper no. 70. Ottawa: Research Centre, Ottawa Board of Education, (mimeo).

HILDEBRAND, J.F.T. 1974a, French immersion pilot program in Fredericton. *Canadian Modern Language Review*, 31, 181–191.

HILDEBRAND, J.F.T. 1974b, The Fredericton plan and how it started: Early French immersion. *Education Canada*, 14, 39–43.

HOPWOOD, A.L. 1974, Year-one evaluation of l'école bilingue. Research Report 74-19. Vancouver, B.C.: Department of Evaluation and Research, Board of School Trustees, (mimeo).

HORNBY, P.A. 1980, Achieving second language fluency through immersion education. *Foreign Language Annals*, 13, 107–113.

*IRELAND, D., GUNNELL, K., & SANTERRE, L. 1980, A study of the teaching and learning of aural/oral French in immersion classes. Ottawa: Ottawa Valley Centre, Ontario Institute for Studies in Education, (mimeo).

KAMIN, J. 1980, Difficulties in early French immersion: A transfer study. Toronto: Ontario Institute for Studies in Education, (mimeo).

KAUFMAN, D. 1974, Longitudinal evaluation of French immersion programs in Coquitlam school district: Report of year one. Burnaby, B.C.: Simon Fraser University, (mimeo).

KAUFMAN, D., & BOSSHARD, B. 1979, Evaluation of the French immersion programs in School District No. 61 (Victoria). Burnaby, B.C.: (mimeo).

KAUFMAN, D., & WILTON, F. 1975, Primary kids do everything in French. *B.C. Teacher*, 55, 54–56.

KLINCK, P. 1980/81, What you always wanted to ask about immersion and were afraid to know! *Alberta Modern Language Journal*, 19(2), 21–27.

*KRASHEN, S. 1980, The theoretical and practical relevance of simple codes in second language. In R. SCARCELLA & S. KRASHEN (eds), *Research in Second Language Acquisition*. Rowley, Mass.: Newbury House.

*KRASHEN, S. 1981, Bilingual education and second language acquisition theory. In Office of Bilingual Bicultural Education (ed.), *Schooling and Language Minority Students: A Theoretical Framework*. Los Angeles, Calif.: Evaluation, Dissemination and Assessment Center, California State University, 51–79.

LAMBERT, W.E. 1974a, Culture and language as factors in learning and education. In F.E. ABOUD & R.D. MEADE (eds), *Cultural Factors in Learning and Education*. Fifth Western Symposium of Learning, 91–122.

LAMBERT, W.E. 1974b, A Canadian experiment in the development of bilingual competence. *Canadian Modern Language Review*, 31, 108–116.

*LAMBERT, W.E. 1975, Culture and language as factors in learning and education. In A. WOLFGANG (ed.), *Education of Immigrant Students*. Toronto, Ontario: Ontario Institute for Studies in Education, 55–83.

LAMBERT, W.E. 1977, The effects of bilingualism on the individual: Cognitive and sociocultural consequences. In P.A. HORNBY (ed.), *Bilingualism: Psychological, Social and Educational Implications*. New York: Academic Press, 15–27.

LAMBERT, W.E. 1978, Cognitive and socio-cultural consequences of bilingualism. *Canadian Modern Language Review*, 34, 537–547.

*LAMBERT, W.E., JUST, M., & SEGALOWITZ, N. 1970, Some cognitive consequences of following the curricula of the early school grades in a foreign language. In J.E. ALATIS (ed.), *Monograph Series on Languages and Linguistics*, vol. 23. Washington, D.C.: Georgetown University Press, 229–279.

*LAMBERT, W.E., & MACNAMARA, J. 1969, Some cognitive consequences of following a first-grade curriculum in a second language. *Journal of Educational Psychology*, 60, 86–96.

*LAMBERT, W.E., & TUCKER, G.R. 1972, *Bilingual Education of Children*. Rowley, Mass.: Newbury House.

LAMBERT, W.E., & TUCKER, G.R. 1977, A home/school language switch program. In W.F. MACKEY & T. ANDERSSON (eds), *Bilingualism in Early Childhood*. Rowley, Mass.: Newbury House, 327–332.

LAMBERT, W.E., & TUCKER, G.R. 1979, Graduates of early immersion: Retrospective views of grade 11 students and their parents. In A. OBADIA (ed.), *Proceedings of the Canadian Association of Immersion Teachers Second National Convention*. Ottawa: Canadian Association of Immersion Teachers, 23–33.

LAMBERT, W.E., TUCKER, G.R., & D'ANGLEJAN, A. 1973a, Cognitive and attitudinal consequences of bilingual schooling: The St. Lambert project through grade five. *Journal of Educational Psychology*, 65, 141–159.

LAMBERT, W.E., TUCKER, G.R., & D'ANGLEJAN, A. 1973b, An innovative approach to second language learning: The St. Lambert experiment. *Etudes de Linguistiques Appliquée*, 10, 90–99.

LANDRY, R. 1980, Les Acadiens sont-ils des semilingues: Quelques réflections à partir de théories existantes sur le bilinguisme. Moncton, N.B.: Université de Moncton, (mimeo).

LAPKIN, S. 1978/79, Bilingual education in Ontario: Issues and directions. *Interchange*, 9, 11–19.

LAPKIN, S. 1979, An analysis of French verb errors made by second language learners in a bilingual program. *Studies in Second Language Acquisition*, 2, 65–84.

LAPKIN, S. 1982a, in press, The English writing skills of French immersion pupils at grade five. *Canadian Modern Language Review*.

LAPKIN, S. 1982b, L'enseignement du français par immersion aux niveaux primaire et secondaire. In P.R. LÉON & J. YASHINSKY (eds), *Options nouvelles en didactique du français langue étrangère*. Montreal, Que.: Didier, 155–162.

*LAPKIN, S., ANDREW, C.M., HARLEY, B., SWAIN, M., & KAMIN, J. 1981, The immersion centre and the dual-track school: A study of the relationship between school environment and achievement in a French immersion program. *Canadian Journal of Education*, 6, 68–90.

LAPKIN, S., & STINSON, R. 1978, Learning in French for half the day. *Orbit*, 42, 3–7.

*LAPKIN, S., & SWAIN, M. 1977, The use of English and French cloze tests in a bilingual education program evaluation: Validity and error analysis. *Language Learning*, 27, 279–314.

LAPKIN, S., SWAIN, M., KAMIN, J., & HANNA, G. 1982, in press, Late immersion in perspective: The Peel study. *Canadian Modern Language Review*.

LEBACH, S. 1974, Report on the Culver City Spanish immersion program in its third year: Its implications for language and subject matter acquisition, language use and attitudes. M.A. thesis, University of California at Los Angeles.

*LEPICQ, D. 1980, Aspects théoriques et empiriques de l'acceptabilité linguistique: Le cas du français des élèves des classes d'immersion. Ph.D. thesis, University of Toronto.

LEWIS, R.F. 1978, An evaluation of the Sydney grade one French immersion program: Final report. Halifax, N.S.: Atlantic Institute of Education, (mimeo).

LEWIS, R.F. 1979a, The valuation of the Halifax grade one French immersion program: Final report. Halifax, N.S.: Atlantic Institute of Education, (mimeo).

LEWIS, R.F. 1979b, The evaluation of the grade 4 and grade 5 program in the French immersion classes of the Unit 3 school board. Halifax, N.S.: Atlantic Institute of Education, (mimeo).

LEWIS, R.F. 1979c, The evaluation of the Sydney grade two French immersion program: Final report. Halifax, N.S.: Atlantic Institute of Education, (mimeo).

LEWIS, R.F., & MURWIN, S. 1978, An evaluation of the Halifax primary French immersion program: Final report. Halifax, N.S.: Atlantic Institute of Education, (mimeo).

*LIEBERSON, S. 1970, *Language and Ethnic Relations in Canada*. New York: Wiley.

LUNDLIE, M., RUMMENS, D., & WESTON, M. 1979, An evaluation of the first eight years of bilingual education at St. Pius X School, Regina, Saskatchewan (Summary). Regina, Sask.: University of Regina, (mimeo).

*MacDonald, E. 1980, An evaluation study of the Unit 3 late immersion program, Prince Edward Island. Charlottetown, P.E.I.: University of P.E.I., (mimeo).

McDougall, A., & Bruck, M. 1976, English reading within the French immersion program: A comparison of the effects of the introduction of English reading at different grade levels. *Language Learning*, 26, 37–43.

*McEachern, W. 1980, Parental decision for French immersion: A look at some influencing factors. *Canadian Modern language Review*, 36, 238–246.

McGillivray, W.R. 1978, The French immersion centre. *Canadian Modern Language Review*, 34, 895–897.

McGillivray, W.R. 1979, Administrative problems of early French immersion. In B. Mlacak & E. Isabelle (eds), *So You Want Your Child to Learn French!* Ottawa, Ont.: Canadian Parents for French, 106–110.

McInnis, C.E. 1976, Three studies of experimental French programs. *Canadian Modern Language Review*, 33, 151–161.

McInnis, C.E., & Donoghue, E.E. 1974, Research and evaluation of second language programs: Final report 1973–74. Ottawa: University of Ottawa, (mimeo).

McInnis, C.E., & Donoghue, E.E. 1975, Research and evaluation of second language programs: Final report 1974–75. Ottawa: University of Ottawa, (mimeo).

McInnis, C.E., & Donoghue, E.E. 1976a, *Report on Research and Evaluation of Second Language Programs, Carleton Roman Catholic School Board, 1975–76.* Toronto: Ministry of Education, Ontario.

McInnis, C.E., & Donoghue, E.E. 1976b, Summary and synthesis of research findings on French language programs in the Carleton Roman Catholic School Board over a three-year period: 1974–76. *Canadian Modern Language Review*, 33, 151–156.

McInnis, C.E., & Donoghue, E.E. 1977, *Research and Evaluation of Second Language Programs in Carleton Separate School Board.* Toronto: Ministry of Education, Ontario.

McInnis, C.E., & Donoghue, E.E. 1978, Research and evaluation of second language programs, final report 1977–78. Ottawa: University of Ottawa, (mimeo).

McInnis, C.E., & Donoghue, E.E. 1980, A comparative study of the relative effectiveness of two different second language training programs. *Canadian Journal of Psychology*, 34, 314–327.

Mackey, W.F. 1975, Le bilinguisme canadien: Bibliographie analytique et guide du chercheur. Quebec, P.Q.: CIRB.

Mackey, W.F. 1978a, Bilingual education policies: Their implications and implementation. *English Quarterly*, 11, 67–94.

Mackey, W.F. 1978b, The importation of bilingual education models. In J.E. Alatis (ed.), *International Dimensions of Bilingual Education. Georgetown Monographs on Languages and Linguistics 1978*. Washington D.C.: Georgetown University Press, 1–18.

Mackey, W.F. 1981, Safeguarding language in schools. *Language and Society*, 4, 10–14.

Mackey, W.F., & Andersson, T. (eds) 1977, *Bilingualism in Early Childhood.* Rowley, Mass.: Newbury House.

MACKEY, W.F., & BEEBE, VON N. (eds) 1977, *Bilingual Schools for a Bicultural Community*. Rowley, Mass.: Newbury House.

MACNAB, G.L., & UNITT, J. 1978, *A Cost Analysis Model For Programs in French as a Second Language*. Toronto: Ministry of Education, Ontario.

MACNAMARA, J. 1972, Perspectives on bilingual education in Canada. *Canadian Psychologist*, 13, 341–349.

*MACNAMARA, J. 1974, What can we expect of a bilingual programme? *Working Papers on Bilingualism*, 4, 42–56.

MACNAMARA, J., EDWARDS, H.P., & BAIN, B. 1978, The "balance effect". *Canadian Modern Language Review*, 34, 890–894.

MACNAMARA, J., HORNER, S., & SVARC, J. 1976, Attending a primary school of the other language in Montreal. In A. SIMOES (ed.), *The Bilingual Child*. New York: Academic Press, 113–131.

MALBOEUF, R. 1978, Vue d'ensemble du programme d'enseignement par immersion partielle (français, langue seconde) au Conseil Scolaire Lakeshore. *Canadian Modern Language Review*, 34, 898–900.

MARESCHAL, R. 1974, Quelques implications de la mise en oeuvre d'un programme de langue seconde. *Canadian Modern Language Review*, 31, 130–141.

MARKMAN, B.R., SPILKA, I.V., & TUCKER, G.R. 1975, The use of elicited imitation in search of an interim French grammar. *Language Learning*, 25, 31–41.

MASSEY, D.A., & POTTER, J. (eds) 1979, *Canadian Parents for French: A Bibliography of Articles and Books on Bilingualism in Education*. Ottawa: Canadian Parents for French.

MAURICE, L.J., & RAY, R.R. 1976, A measurement of bilinguality achieved in immersion programs. *Canadian Modern Language Review*, 32, 575–582.

MES-PRAT, M., & EDWARDS, H.P. 1981, Elementary French immersion children's use of orthographic structure for reading. *Canadian Modern Language Review*, 37, 682–693.

MLACAK, B., & ISABELLE, E. (eds) 1979, *So You Want Your Child to Learn French!* Ottawa: Canadian Parents for French.

MORRISON, F., BONYUN, R., KIRBY, D.M., MARTIN, J.C., PAWLEY, C., RIEL, Y., & WIGHTMAN, M. 1977, Longitudinal Evaluations of Alternative Programs for Teaching French as a Second Language: Evaluation of the Federally and Provincially Funded Extensions of the Second Language Learning (French) Programs in the Schools of the Ottawa and Carleton Boards of Education. Fourth Annual Report. Ottawa: Research Centre, Ottawa Board of Education, (mimeo).

*MORRISON, F., BONYUN, R., PAWLEY, C., & WALSH, M. 1979, *French Proficiency Status of Ottawa and Carleton Students in Alternative Programs: Evaluation of the Second Language Learning (French) Programs in the Schools of the Ottawa and Carleton Board of Education*. Sixth Annual Report. Toronto: Ministry of Education, Ontario.

MORRISON, F., KIRBY, D.M., MACNAB, G.L., PAWLEY, C.A., WALSH, M.D., & WIGHTMAN, M. 1978, Alternative Programs for Teaching French as a Second Language: Research and Evaluation: Evaluation of the Extensions of the Second Language Learning (French) Programs in the Schools of the Ottawa and Carleton Boards of Education. Fifth Annual Report. Ottawa: Research Centre, Ottawa Board of Education, Ontario, (mimeo).

MORRISON, M.L., 1979, French immersion: How to keep it. In B. MLACAK & E. ISABELLE (eds), *So You Want Your Child to Learn French!* Ottawa: Canadian Parents for French, 103-105.

MULLER, L.J., PENNER, W.J., BLOWERS, T.A., JONES, J.P., & MOSYCHUK, H. 1977, Evaluation of a bilingual (English-Ukrainian) program. *Canadian Modern Language Review*, 33, 476-485.

*MYKLEBUST, H.R. 1971, *The Pupil Rating Scale*. New York: Grune and Stratton.

NAIMAN, N. 1973, Imitation, comprehension, and production of certain syntactic forms by young children acquiring a second language. Ph.D. thesis, University of Toronto.

NAIMAN, N. 1974, The use of elicited imitation in second language acquisition research. *Working Papers on Bilingualism*, 2, 1-37.

NETTEN, J.E., GLEASON, T.P., HEFFERNAN, P., PRINCE, M.A., & KOSKI, G.R. 1976, An evaluation report of the Port au Port immersion project kindergarten year 1975-76 in Cape St. George, Newfoundland. St. John's: Memorial University of Newfoundland, (mimeo).

NETTEN, J.E., & SPAIN, W.H. 1979, An evaluation of some aspects of the French bilingual education programme conducted by the St. John's Roman Catholic School Board. St. John's, Nfld.: Institute for Educational Research and Development, Memorial University of Newfoundland and the Roman Catholic School Board for St. John's, (mimeo).

NETTEN, J.E., SPAIN, W.H., & HEFFERNAN, P. 1977, An evaluation report of the Port au Port immersion project for the year 1976-77 in Cape St. George, Newfoundland. St. John's and Stephenville: Memorial University of Newfoundland and The Port au Port Roman Catholic Separate School Board, (mimeo).

OBADIA, A.A. (ed.) 1979, *Proceedings of the C.A.I.T. Second National Convention: The Pupil in an Immersion Programme*. Ottawa: Canadian Association of Immersion Teachers/Association canadienne des professeurs d'immersion.

OLIVER, E., BROWN, G., & MCKENZIE, C. 1975, Wellington County French immersion program: Kindergarten and grade 1. Guelph, Ont.: Wellington County Board of Education, (mimeo).

OLIVER, E., CORLETT, C., & MCKENZIE, C. 1976, Wellington County French immersion program: Kindergarten and grade 1, 1975-76. Guelph, Ont.: Wellington County Board of Education, (mimeo).

*OLLER, J.W., Jr. 1979, *Language Tests at School*: London: Longman.

PARISEAU, C. 1978, Experience dans une classe d'immersion française aux Mille-Iles. *Canadian Modern Language Review*, 34, 904-905.

PARKER, D.V. 1973, Planning an immersion program in French. *Elements*, 5, 5-6.

PARTLOW, H.R. 1977, *The Costs of Providing Instruction in French to Students Studying French as a Second Language*. Toronto: Ministry of Education, Ontario.

PENNEY, W. 1979, Report of the French immersion kindergarten program at Gander Academy Primary (1978-79). Gander, Nfld.: Terra Nova Integrated School Board, (mimeo).

PENNEY, W. 1980, Report of the French immersion program at Gander Academy Primary (1979-80). Gander, Nfld.: Terra Nova Integrated School Board, (mimeo).

PFEIFFER, M.G. 1979, An evaluation study of the grade VI bilingual programme in School District No. 35 (Langley) 1978–79. Langley, B.C.: School District No. 35 (Langley), (mimeo).

POLICH, E. 1973a, Evaluation of the 1971–72 grade eight and the 1972–73 grade nine French immersion programs. Montreal: Protestant School Board of Greater Montreal, (mimeo).

POLICH, E. 1973b, Report on the evaluation of the grade seven French immersion program 1971–72. Montreal: Protestant School Board of Greater Montreal, (mimeo).

POLICH, E. 1973c, Report on the evaluation of the lower elementary French immersion program through grade three, 1971–73. Montreal: Protestant School Board of Greater Montreal, (mimeo).

POLITZER, R. 1976, Initial language acquisition in two bilingual schools. *Working Papers on Bilingualism*, 10, 1–21.

PROTESTANT SCHOOL BOARD OF GREATER MONTREAL 1971, Grade seven 1970–71 French immersion project. Student Personnel Services and Curriculum Department, (mimeo).

PROTESTANT SCHOOL BOARD OF GREATER MONTREAL. 1972, Report on the 1971–72 Roslyn French immersion results, (mimeo).

PROTESTANT SCHOOL BOARD OF GREATER MONTREAL. 1973a, Evaluation of the 1972–73 grade eleven French immersion programme, (mimeo).

PROTESTANT SCHOOL BOARD OF GREATER MONTREAL. 1973b, Assessment of grade three students who enrolled from English kindergarten into the grade one French immersion program, (mimeo).

PROTESTANT SCHOOL BOARD OF GREATER MONTREAL. 1973c, Report on the 1972–73 Roslyn French immersion evaluation, (mimeo).

PROTESTANT SCHOOL BOARD OF GREATER MONTREAL. 1975, Evaluation of the 1972–73 grade ten French immersion students, (mimeo).

*PYCOCK, C.J. 1977, The effectiveness of two approaches used to introduce English in grade two bilingual classes. Montreal, Que.: South Shore Protestant Regional School Board, (mimeo).

*RICHARDS, M.K. 1978, A comparison of classroom climate in regular and French immersion classes. Ph.D. thesis, University of Toronto.

RICHER, S., & HUGHES, F. 1977, French immersion and classroom behaviour: A new direction for research in second language learning. Ottawa: Carleton University, (mimeo).

SAMUELS, M., REYNOLDS, A.G., & LAMBERT, W.E. 1969, Communicational efficiency of children schooled in a foreign language. *Journal of Educational Psychology*, 60, 389–393.

SELINKER, L., SWAIN, M., & DUMAS, G. 1975, The interlanguage hypothesis extended to children. *Language Learning*, 25, 139–152.

SHAPSON, S.M. 1978, Longitudinal evaluation of the early-entry immersion programs in Coquitlam School District (No. 43): Report to the end of grade 4. Burnaby, B.C.: Faculty of Education, Simon Fraser University, (mimeo).

SHAPSON, S.M., & BOSSHARD, B. 1980, Evaluation of the French immersion program in School District No. 61 (Victoria): Report of phase II. Burnaby, B.C.: Faculty of Education, Simon Fraser University, (mimeo).

SHAPSON, S.M., & DAY, E. 1978, A study of the 1978 grade 10 late immersion program in Coquitlam School District (No. 43). Burnaby, B.C.: Faculty of Education, Simon Fraser University, (mimeo).

108   EVALUATING BILINGUAL EDUCATION

SHAPSON, S.M., & DAY, E. 1979a, The North Shore early-immersion program: Report on the kindergarten year (1978–79). Burnaby, B.C.: Faculty of Education, Simon Fraser University, (mimeo).

SHAPSON, S.M., & DAY, E. 1979b, The Burnaby early-immersion program: Report on the 1978–1979 school year. Burnaby, B.C.: Faculty of Education, Simon Fraser University, (mimeo).

SHAPSON, S.M., & DAY, E. 1979c, Evaluation study of the late immersion program: School District No. 43 (Coquitlam) grade 6 1978–79. Burnaby, B.C.: Faculty of Education, Simon Fraser University, (mimeo).

SHAPSON, S.M., & DAY, E. 1979d, Evaluation study of the late immersion programs: Surrey School District (grade 6, 1978–79). Burnaby, B.C.: Faculty of Education, Simon Fraser University, (mimeo).

SHAPSON, S.M., & DAY, E. 1979e, A study of the 1979 high school immersion program in School District No. 43 (Coquitlam). Burnaby, B.C.: Faculty of Education, Simon Fraser University, (mimeo).

SHAPSON, S.M., & DAY, E. 1980, Longitudinal evaluation of the early-entry immersion program in Coquitlam School District: Report to the end of Year 6. Burnaby, B.C.: Faculty of Education, Simon Fraser University, (mimeo).

SHAPSON, S.M., & KAUFMAN, D. 1975, Longitudinal evaluation of French immersion programs in Coquitlam school district: Report of year II. Burnaby, B.C.: Simon Fraser University, (mimeo).

SHAPSON, S.M., & KAUFMAN, D. 1976a, The Coquitlam late immersion experiment in junior secondary school. Burnaby, B.C.: Simon Fraser University, (mimeo).

SHAPSON, S.M., & KAUFMAN, D. 1976b, French immersion: A western perspective: Issues and research. *Canadian Society for the Study of Education*, 3, 8–26.

SHAPSON, S.M., & KAUFMAN, D. 1978a, Overview of elementary French programs in British Columbia: Issues and Research. *Canadian Modern Language Review*, 34, 586–603.

*SHAPSON, S.M., & KAUFMAN, D. 1978b, A study of a late immersion French program in secondary school. *Canadian Modern Language Review*, 34, 186–193.

SHAPSON, S.M., & KAUFMAN, D. 1978c, Overview of secondary and post-secondary French immersion: Issues and research. *The Canadian Modern Language Review*, 34, 604–620.

SHAPSON, S.M., & PURBHOO, M. 1974, Second language programs for young children. Toronto: Board of Education for the City of Toronto, Research Department, no. 122, (mimeo).

*SNOW, C., & FERGUSON, C. (eds) 1977, *Talking to Children: Language Input and Acquisition*. Cambridge: At the University Press.

SPAIN, W.H., & NETTEN, J.E. 1978, An evaluation of some aspects of the French bilingual education programme conducted by the St. John's Roman Catholic School Board (1977–78). St. John's, Nfld.: Memorial University and Roman Catholic School Board of St. John's, (mimeo).

SPAIN, W.H., & NETTEN, J.E. 1980, Avalon Consolidated School Board late immersion French project, 1979–80. Summary of Findings: A preliminary report. St. John's, Nfld.: Memorial University, (mimeo).

SPAIN, W.H., NETTEN, J.E., & SHEPPARD, A.W. 1980, Background characteristics: Opinions and attitudes of parents electing an early French immersion programme for their children. St. John's, Nfld. and Stephenville, Nfld.: Institute for Educational Research and Development, Memorial University and Port-au-Port Roman Catholic School Board, (mimeo).

SPAIN, W.H., NETTEN, J.E., & WATSON, D. 1979, The relationship of French comprehension to English language measures of reading readiness, reading and mathematics achievement, and language development in a rural, French immersion programme. Paper presented at CERA Annual Conference, Saskatoon, Sask., (mimeo).

SPILKA, I.V. 1976, Evaluating spontaneous speech production in a second language. In W. von Raffler-Engel and Y. LEBRUN (eds), *Baby Talk and Infant Speech.* Amsterdam, The Netherlands: Swets and Zeitlinger B.V.

SPILKA, I.V. 1976, Assessment of second language performance in immersion programs. *Canadian Modern Language Review,* 32, 543–561.

SPILKA, I.V. 1979, Apprentissage du pronom 'en'. *Vingt-cinq ans de linguistique au Canada: Hommages à Jean-Paul Vinay.* Montreal: Centre éducatif et culturel.

STANLEY, M.H. 1974, French immersion programs: The experience of the Protestant School Board of Greater Montreal. *Canadian Modern Language Review,* 31, 152–160.

STANUTZ, S. 1974, The teaching of French as a second language in Ottawa. *Canadian Modern Language Review,* 31, 142–151.

STERN, H.H. 1973a, Bilingual schooling and second language teaching: A review of recent North American experience. In J.W. OLLER & J.C. RICHARDS (eds), *Focus on the Learner: Pragmatic Perspectives for the Language Teacher.* Rowley, Mass.: Newbury House, 274–282.

STERN, H.H. 1973b, Bilingual education: A review of recent North American experience. *Modern Languages,* 54, 57–62.

STERN, H.H. 1978a, Bilingual schooling and foreign language education: Some implications of Canadian experiments in French immersion. In J.E. ALATIS (ed.), *International Dimensions of Bilingual Education. Georgetown University Round Table on Languages and Linguistics 1978.* Washington, D.C.: Georgetown University Press, 165–188.

STERN, H.H. 1978b, Language research and the classroom practitioner. *Canadian Modern Language Review,* 34, 680–687.

STERN, H.H. 1978c, French immersion in Canada: Achievements and directions. *Canadian Modern Language Review,* 34, 836–854.

STERN, H.H. 1978d, The formal-functional distinction in language pedagogy: A conceptual clarification. Paper presented at the Fifth International Congress of Applied Linguistics, Montreal, (mimeo).

STERN, H.H. 1980, Some approaches to communicative language teaching in Canada. Proceedings of ACTFL Conference, October 1979. *Studies in Second Language Acquisition,* 3, 57–63.

STERN, H.H., & SWAIN, M. 1974, Notes on language learning in bilingual kindergarten classes. In G. RONDEAU (ed.), *Current Trends in Canadian Applied Linguistics.* Montreal: Centre educatif et culturel.

STERN, H.H., SWAIN, M., & McLEAN, L.D. 1976a, *French Programs: Some Major Issues.* Toronto, Ont.: Ministry of Education, Ontario.

*STERN, H.H., SWAIN, M., McLEAN, L.D., FRIEDMAN, R.J., HARLEY, B., & LAPKIN, S. 1976b, *Three Approaches to Teaching French: Evaluation and Overview of Studies Related to the Federally-Funded Extensions of the Second Language Learning (French) Programs in the Carleton and Ottawa School Boards.* Toronto, Ministry of Education, Ontario.

STERN, H.H., & WEINRIB, A. 1978, Foreign languages for younger children: Trends and assessment. In V. KINSELLA (ed.), *Language Teaching and Linguistics: Surveys*. Cambridge: Cambridge University Press, 152–172.

SWAIN, M. 1972a, Bilingualism as a first language. Ph.D. thesis, University of California at Irvine.

SWAIN, M. (ed.) 1972b, *Bilingual Schooling: Some Experiences in Canada and the United States*. Toronto, Ont.: Ontario Institute for Studies in Education.

SWAIN, M. 1974a, French immersion programs across Canada: Research findings. *Canadian Modern Language Review*, 31, 117–129.

SWAIN, M. 1974b, Child bilingual language learning and linguistic interdependence. In S. CAREY (ed.), *Bilingualism, Biculturalism and Education*. Edmonton: University of Alberta Press, 75–81.

*SWAIN, M. 1975a, Writing skills of grade three French immersion pupils. *Working Papers on Bilingualism*, 7, 1–38.

SWAIN, M. 1975b, More about primary French immersion classes. *Orbit*, 27, 13–15.

SWAIN, M. 1976a, Some issues in bilingual education in Canada. In A. VALDMAN (ed.), *Identité Culturelle et Francophonie dans les Ameriques*. Quebec: Presses de l'Université Laval, 37–43.

SWAIN, M. 1976b, Changes in errors: Random or systematic? In G. NICKEL (ed.), *Proceedings of the Fourth International Congress of Applied Linguistics*, vol. 2, Stuttgart: Hochschulverlag, 345–358.

SWAIN, M. 1976c, English-speaking child + early French immersion = bilingual child? *Canadian Modern Language Review*, 33, 180–187.

SWAIN, M. 1977a, Bilingualism: Some non-political issues. *Multiculturalism*, 1, 13–16.

SWAIN, M. 1977b, Bilingualism through education: Dreams and realities. *Manitoba Modern Language Bulletin*, 11, 3–10.

SWAIN, M. 1977c, Bilingualism, monolingualism and code acquisition. In: W.F. MACKEY & T. ANDERSSON (eds), *Bilingualism in Early Childhood*. Rowley, Mass.: Newbury House, 28–35.

SWAIN, M. 1977d, Future directions in second language research. In *Proceedings of the Los Angeles Second Language Acquisition Forum*, ESL Section, UCLA, 15–28.

*SWAIN, M. 1978a, French immersion: Early, late or partial? *Canadian Modern Language Review*, 34, 577–585.

SWAIN, M. 1978b, Home-school language switching. In J. RICHARDS (ed.), *Understanding Second and Foreign Language Learning: Issues and Approaches*. Rowley, Mass.: Newbury House, 238–251.

*SWAIN, M. 1978c, Bilingual education for the English-Canadian. In J.E. ALATIS (ed.), *International Dimensions of Bilingual Education. Georgetown University Round Table on Languages and Linguistics 1978*. Washington, D.C.: Georgetown University Press, 141–154.

SWAIN, M. 1978d, School reform through bilingual education: Problems and some solutions in evaluating programs. In J. SIMMONS & R.G. PAULSTON (eds), *Comparative Education Review*, Oct., 420–433.

SWAIN, M. 1979a, Bilingual education: Research and its implications. In C.A. YORIO, K. PERKINS, & J. SCHACHTER (eds), *On TESOL '79: The Learner in Focus*. Washington, D.C.: TESOL, 23–33.

SWAIN, M. 1979b, What does research say about immersion education? In B. MLACAK & E. ISABELLE (eds), *So You Want Your Child to Learn French!* Ottawa: Canadian Parents for French, 20–27.

SWAIN, M. 1979c, L2 and content learning: A Canadian bilingual education program at the secondary grade levels. In E. BRIÈRE (ed.), *Language Development in a Bilingual Setting*. Los Angeles: National Dissemination and Assessment Center, 113–120.

*SWAIN, M. 1980a, French immersion programs in Canada. *Multiculturalism*, 4(2), 3–6.

SWAIN, M. 1980b, Bilingual education for the English-Canadian: Three models of "immersion". *Bilingual Education Anthology Series 7*. Singapore: RELC, 7, 19–36.

SWAIN, M. 1981a, Target language use in the wider environment as a factor in its acquisition. In R. ANDERSEN (ed.), *New Dimensions in Second Language Acquisition Research*. Rowley, Mass.: Newbury House, 109–123.

*SWAIN, M. 1981b, Linguistic expectations: Core, extended, and immersion. *Canadian Modern Language Review*, 37(3), 486–497.

SWAIN, M. 1981c, Time and timing in bilingual education. *Language Learning*, 31, 1–15.

*SWAIN, M. 1981d, Immersion education: Applicability for nonvernacular teaching to vernacular speakers. *Studies in Second Language Acquisition*, 4, 1–17.

*SWAIN, M. 1982, Bilingualism without tears. Paper presented at the 16th Annual International Convention of TESOL, Honolulu, Hawaii.

SWAIN, M., & BARIK, H.C. 1973, French immersion classes: A promising route to bilingualism. *Orbit*, 4, 3–5.

SWAIN, M., & BARIK, H.C. 1976a, A large scale program in French immersion: The Ottawa study through grade three. *ITL. A Review of Applied Linguistics*, 33, 1–25.

SWAIN, M., & BARIK, H.C. 1976b, *Five Years of Primary French Immersion: Annual Reports of the Bilingual Education Project to the Carleton Board of Education and the Ottawa Board of Education up to 1975*. Toronto, Ont.: Ministry of Education, Ontario.

SWAIN, M., & BARIK, H.C. 1976c, Bilingual education for the English-Canadian: Recent developments. In A. SIMOES (ed.), *The Bilingual Child: Research and Analysis of Existing Educational Themes*. New York: Academic Press, 91–111.

SWAIN, M., & BARIK, H.C. 1977, Report to Ottawa Board of Education and Carleton Board of Education re: Evaluation of the 1976–77 French immersion program in grades 4–6. Toronto, Ont.: Ontario Institute for Studies in Education, (mimeo).

SWAIN, M., & BARIK, H.C. 1978a, The role of curricular approach, rural-urban background, and socio-economic status in second language learning: The Cornwall area study. *Alberta Journal of Educational Research*, 24, 1–16.

SWAIN, M., & BARIK, H.C. 1978b, Bilingual education in Canada: French and English. In B. SPOLSKY & R.L. COOPER (eds), *Case Studies in Bilingual Education*. Rowley, Mass.: Newbury House, 22–71.

SWAIN, M., & BRUCK, M. (guest eds) 1976, Proceedings of the research conference on immersion education for the majority child. *Canadian Modern Language Review*, 32, entire no. 5.

SWAIN, M., & BURNABY, B. 1976, Personality characteristics and second language learning in young children: A pilot study. *Working Papers on Bilingualism*, 11, 115–128.

*SWAIN, M., & CUMMINS, J. 1979, Bilingualism, cognitive functioning and education. *Language Teaching and Linguistics: Abstracts*, 4–18.

SWAIN, M., DUMAS, G., & NAIMAN, N. 1974, Alternatives to spontaneous speech: Elicited translation and imitation as indicators of second language competence. *Working Papers on Bilingualism*, 3, 68–79.

*SWAIN, M., & LAPKIN, S. 1977, Beginning French immersion at grade 8. *Orbit*, 39, 10–13.

SWAIN, M., LAPKIN, S., & ANDREW, C.M. 1981, Early French immersion later on. *Journal of Multilingual and Multicultural Development*, 2, 1–23.

*SWAIN, M., LAPKIN, S., & BARIK, H.C. 1976, The cloze test as a measure of second language proficiency for young children. *Working Papers on Bilingualism*, 11, 32–42.

SWAIN, M., LAPKIN, S., & HANNA, G. 1980, Report to the Elgin County Board of Education on the 1979 evaluation of the partial French immersion program in grade 4, 7 and 8. Toronto, Ont.: Ontario Institute for Studies in Education, (mimeo).

SWAIN, M., & NAIMAN, N. 1976, Discussion of second language acquisition research: Getting a more global look at the learner. In H.D. BROWN (ed.), *Papers in Second Language Acquisition*; special issue of *Language Learning*, 4, 29–38.

SWAIN, M., NAIMAN, N., & DUMAS, G. 1978, Aspects of the learning of French by English-speaking five year olds. In E. HATCH (ed.), *Second Language Acquisition*. Rowley, Mass.: Newbury House, 297–309.

SWAIN, M., & WESCHE, M. 1975, Linguistic interaction: Case study of a bilingual child. *Language Sciences*, 37, 17–22.

*SWAIN, M., WESCHE, M., & MACHIN, J. 1972, French immersion kindergarten program in capital area schools: Analysis of interviews with parents and pupils. Toronto: Ontario Institute for Studies in Education, (mimeo).

SWEET, R.J. 1974, The pilot immersion program at Allenby Public School, Toronto. *Canadian Modern Language Review*, 31, 161–168.

*SZAMOSI, M., SWAIN, M., & LAPKIN, S. 1979, Do early immersion pupils 'know' French? *Orbit*, 49, 20–23.

TARONE, E., FRAUENFELDER, U., & SELINKER, L. 1976, Systematicity/Variability and stability/instability in interlanguage systems: More data from Toronto French immersion. In H.D. BROWN (ed.), *Papers in Second Language Acquisition*, special issue of *Language Learning*, 4, 93–134.

TARONE, E., SWAIN, M., & FATHMAN, A. 1976, Some limitations to the classroom applications of current second language acquisition research. *TESOL Quarterly*, 10, 19–32.

TOMKO, T. 1975, Ukrainian-English bilingual evaluation 1974–75. Edmonton, Alta.: Edmonton Catholic School Board, (mimeo).

TRITES, R.L. 1976a, Difficulties in early French immersion. In E. ISABELLE (ed.), *What's What for Children Learning French*. Ottawa, Ont.: Mutual Press, 29–32.

TRITES, R.L. 1976b, Children with learning difficulties in primary French immersion. *Canadian Modern Language Review*, 33, 193–216.

TRITES, R.L. 1978, Learning disabilities in immersion. *Canadian Modern Language Review*, 34, 888–889.

TRITES, R.L. 1979, A reply to Cummins. *Canadian Modern Language Review*, 36, 143–146.

TRITES, R.L. 1981, Primary French Immersion: Disabilities and Prediction of Success. *Review and Evaluation Bulletins*, 2(5). Toronto: Ministry of Education, Ontario.

TRITES, R.L., & PRICE, M.A. 1976, *Learning Disabilities Found in Association with French Immersion Programming*. Toronto: Ministry of Education, Ontario.

TRITES, R.L., & PRICE, M.A. 1977, *Learning Disabilities Found in Association with French Immersion Programming: A Cross Validation*. Toronto: Ministry of Education, Ontario.

TRITES, R.L., & PRICE, M.A. 1978/79, Specific learning disability in primary French immersion. *Interchange*, 9, 73–85.

TRITES, R.L., & PRICE, M.A. 1979, *Assessment of Readiness for Primary French Immersion: Kindergarten Follow-Up Assessment*. Toronto: Ministry of Education, Ontario.

TRITES, R.L., & PRICE, M.A. 1980, *Assessment of Readiness for Primary French Immersion: Grade One Follow-Up Assessment*. Toronto: Ministry of Education, Ontario.

TUCKER, G.R. 1974a, Methods of second language teaching. *Canadian Modern Language Review*, 31, 102–107.

TUCKER, G.R. 1974b, The assessment of bilingual and bicultural factors of communication. In S.T. CAREY (ed.), *Bilingualism, Biculturalism and Education*. Edmonton, Alta: University of Alberta Press, 217–222.

TUCKER, G.R. 1975a, The development of reading skills within a bilingual education program. In S.S. SMILEY & J.C. TOWNER (eds), *Language and Reading*. Bellingham, Wash.: Sixth Western Washington Symposium on Learning, 49–60.

TUCKER, G.R. 1975b, The acquisition of knowledge by children educated bilingually. *Georgetown Monograph Series on Languages and Linguistics*, 267–277.

TUCKER, G.R. 1976, Summary: Research conference on immersion education for the majority child. *Canadian Modern Language Review*, 32, 585–591.

TUCKER, G.R. 1977a, Bilingual education: The linguistic perspective in bilingual education. *Current perspectives*, 2, Arlington, Va.: Center for Applied Linguistics, 1–40.

TUCKER, G.R. 1977b, Some observations concerning bilingualism and second language teaching in developing countries and in North America. In P.A. HORNBY (ed.), *Bilingualism: Psychological, Social and Educational Implications*. New York: Academic Press, 141–146.

TUCKER, G.R. 1979, Bilingual education: Some perplexing observations. *Educational Evaluation and Policy Analysis*, 1, 74–75.

TUCKER, G.R., & D'ANGLEJAN, A. 1971, Some thoughts concerning bilingual education programs. *Modern Language Journal*, 55, 491–493.

TUCKER, G.R., & D'ANGLEJAN, A. 1972, An approach to bilingual education: The St. Lambert experiment. In M. SWAIN (ed.), *Bilingual Schooling: Some Experiences in Canada and the United States*. Toronto: Ontario Institute for Studies in Education, 15–21.

TUCKER, G.R., & D'ANGLEJAN, A. 1975, New directions in second language teaching. In R.C. TROIKE & N. MODIANO (eds), *Proceedings of the First Inter-American Conference on Bilingual Education.* Arlington, Va.: Center for Applied Linguistics, 63–72.

TUCKER, G.R., HAMAYAN, E., & GENESEE, F. 1976, Affective, cognitive and social factors in second language acquisition. *Canadian Modern language Review*, 32, 214–226.

TUCKER, G.R., LAMBERT, W.E., & D'ANGLEJAN, A. 1973, French immersion programs: A pilot investigation. *Language Sciences*, 25, 19–26.

WALDMAN, E.L. 1975, Cross-ethnic attitudes of Anglo students in Spanish immersion bilingual and English schooling. M.A. thesis, University of California at Los Angeles.

*WIGHTMAN, M. 1977, Mathematics achievement of students in experimental French programs. FRENCH Working Paper no. 117. Ottawa, Ont.: Research Centre of the Ottawa Board of Education, (mimeo).

WIGHTMAN, P. 1979, French immersion: An educational alternative. In B. MLACAK & E. ISABELLE (eds), *So You Want Your Child to Learn French!* Ottawa: Canadian Parents for French, 54–65.

WILTON, F. 1974, Implications of a second language program: The Coquitlam experience. *Canadian Modern Language Review*, 31, 169–180.

*WOLSK, D. 1977, Program evaluation: L'école bilingue. Research Report 77-05. Vancouver, B.C.: Evaluation and Research Education Services Group.

Appendix

List of Evaluation Reports: Bilingual Education Project

Carleton Board of Education/Ottawa Board of Education

BARIK, H.C., & SWAIN, M. 1975, Three-year evaluation of a large scale early grade French immersion program: The Ottawa study. *Language Learning*, 25, 1–30.

SWAIN, M., & BARIK, H.C. 1976, A large scale program in French immersion: The Ottawa study through grade three. *ITL, A Review of Applied Linguistics*, 33, 1–25.

BARIK, H.C., & SWAIN, M. 1977, French immersion in Canada: The Ottawa study through grade four. *ITL, A Review of Applied Linguistics*, 36, 45–70.

BARIK, H.C., & SWAIN, M. 1976, Programmes d'immersion en français en Ontario: Résultats d'une étude. *Bulletin de la F.I.P.F.* (Fédération internationale des professeurs de français), 12–13, 75–83.

SWAIN, M., & BARIK, H.C. 1976, *Five Years of Primary French Immersion: Annual Reports of the Bilingual Education Project to the Carleton Board of Education and the Ottawa Board of Education up to 1975*. Toronto: Ministry of Education, Ontario.

SWAIN, M. 1976, English-speaking child + early French immersion = bilingual child? *The Canadian Modern Language Review*, 33, 180–187.

BARIK, H.C., & SWAIN, M. 1978, Evaluation of a French immersion program: The Ottawa study through grade five. *Canadian Journal of Behavioural Science*, 10, 192–201.

SWAIN, M., & BARIK, H.C. 1977, Report to Ottawa Board of Education and Carleton Board of Education re: Evaluation of the 1976–77 French immersion program in grades 4–6. Toronto: The Ontario Institute for Studies in Education, (mimeo).

ANDREW, C.M., LAPKIN, S., & SWAIN, M. 1979, Report on the 1978 evaluation of the Ottawa and Carleton French immersion programs, grades 5–7. Toronto: The Ontario Institute for Studies in Education, (mimeo).

LAPKIN, S., ANDREW, C.M., HARLEY, B., SWAIN, M., & KAMIN, J. 1979, The immersion centre and the dual-track school: A study of the relationship between school environment and achievement in a French immersion program. Toronto: The Ontario Institute for Studies in Education, (mimeo).

SWAIN, M., LAPKIN, S., & ANDREW, C.M. 1981, Early French immersion later on. *Journal of Multilingual and Multicultural Development*, 2, 1–23.

Toronto Board of Education

BARIK, H.C., & SWAIN, M. 1976, Early grade French immersion classes in a unilingual English Canadian setting; The Toronto study. *Scientia Paedagogica Experimentalis*, 12, 153–177.

BARIK, H.C., & SWAIN, M. 1976, Primary-grade French immersion in a unilingual English-Canadian setting: The Toronto study through grade 2. *Canadian Journal of Education*, 1, 39–58.

BARIK, H.C., & SWAIN, M. 1976, Update on French immersion: The Toronto study through grade 3. *Canadian Journal of Education*, 1(4), 33–42.

BARIK, H.C., & SWAIN, M. 1978, Follow-up on French immersion: The Toronto study through grade four. *Scientia Paedagogica Experimentalis*, 15, 181–206.

BARIK, H.C., & SWAIN, M. 1978, Report to the Toronto Board of Education re: Evaluation of the 1976–77 French immersion program in grades 3–5 at Allenby Public School. Toronto: The Ontario Institute for Studies in Education, (mimeo).

ANDREW, C.M., LAPKIN, S., & SWAIN, M. 1979, Report on the 1978 evaluation of the French immersion program at Allenby Public School in Toronto, grades 4–6. Toronto: The Ontario Institute for Studies in Education, (mimeo).

ANDREW, C.M., LAPKIN, S., & SWAIN, M. 1980, Report on the 1979 evaluation of a French immersion program and an extended French program in the Toronto board of Education, grades 5–8. Toronto: The Ontario Institute for Studies in Education, (mimeo).

Elgin County Board of Education

BARIK, H.C., & SWAIN, M. 1974, English-French bilingual education in the early grades: The Elgin study. *Modern Language Journal*, 58, 392–403.

BARIK, H.C., & SWAIN, M. 1976, English-French bilingual education in the early grades: The Elgin study through grade four. *Modern Language Journal*, 60, 3–17.

BARIK, H.C., SWAIN, M., & NWANUNOBI, E. 1977, English-French bilingual education: The Elgin study through grade five. *The Canadian Modern Language Review*, 33, 459–475.

BARIK, H.C., & SWAIN, M. 1978, Evaluation of a bilingual education program in Canada: The Elgin study through grade six. *Bulletin CILA*, 27, 31–58.

BARIK, H.C., & SWAIN, M. 1977, Report to the Elgin County Board of Education re: Evaluation of the 1976–77 partial French immersion program in grades 5–7. Toronto: The Ontario Institute for Studies in Education, (mimeo).

LAPKIN, S., & STINSON, R. 1978, Learning in French for half the day. *Orbit*, 42, 3–7.

ANDREW, C.M., LAPKIN, S., & SWAIN, M. 1979, Report to the Elgin County Board of Education on the 1978 evaluation of the partial French immersion programs in grades 3, 6, 7, and 8. Toronto: The Ontario Institute for Studies in Education, (mimeo).

SWAIN, M., LAPKIN, S., & HANNA, G. 1980, Report to the Elgin County Board of Education on the 1979 evaluation of the partial French immersion programs in grades 4, 7, and 8. Toronto: The Ontario Institute for Studies in Education, (mimeo).

Peel County Board of Education

BARIK, H.C., & SWAIN, M. 1976, A Canadian experiment in bilingual education: The Peel study. *Foreign Language Annals*, 9, 465–479.

BARIK, H.C., SWAIN, M., & GAUDINO, V. 1976, A Canadian experiment in bilingual education in the senior grades: The Peel study through grade 10. *International Review of Applied Psychology*, 25, 99–113.

SWAIN, M. 1979, L2 and content learning: A Canadian bilingual education program at the secondary grade levels. In E. BRIÈRE (ed.), *Language Development in a Bilingual Setting*. Los Angeles: National Dissemination and Assessment Center, 113–120.

SWAIN, M., & LAPKIN, S. 1977, Beginning French immersion at grade 8. *Orbit*, 39, 10–13.

ANDREW, C.M., LAPKIN, S., & SWAIN, M. 1980, Report to the Peel County Board of Education on the 1978 evaluation of the late French immersion (LFI) program in grades 8, 11, 12, and 13. Toronto: The Ontario Institute for Studies in Education, (mimeo).

LAPKIN, S., SWAIN, M., KAMIN, J., & HANNA, G. 1982, in press, Late immersion in perspective: The Peel Study. *Canadian Modern Language Review*.